you *are* loved

a remarakable true story of
God's never-failing grace

nola jean stacey

ARK house

Ark House Press
arkhousepress.com

Cataloguing in Publication Data:
Title: You Are Loved
ISBN: 978-1-7641051-1-8 (pbk)
Subjects: REL012170   RELIGION / Christian Living / Personal Memoirs; REL012040   RELIGION / Christian Living / Inspirational; REL012030 RELIGION / Christian Living / Family & Relationships

Design by initiateagency.com

This is dedicated to my husband Keith and my daughter Kate and son Mark. You are all the wind beneath my wings and my rock thank you.

Table of Contents

———

Foreword

———

What is this? How did it happen? Why has it changed? What is it now? These are four probing questions that I needed to ask myself after the manuscript had been read by a friend, as part of an edit to help me decide what I wanted to do about it? For me reading the initial manuscript, which I had called "Meet My Demons", reminded me where and why the whole thing started, and to how it got its beginnings. In looking back, it's interesting to see just how God works, the saying that He works in "mysterious ways" certainly rings true with me, and with the writing of this story.

Over the years I had fancied myself as somewhat of a writer. I loved writing stuff for the kids at school, and then putting music to it. Cinderella has been one of my favourite fairytales. I wrote it as a Rock Opera, but one that had a Christian flavour. I incorporated many songs, including the opening song, sung to the tune of Neil Diamond's "Crackling Rosie".

Cinderella, how you going to get your fella? Heh! Heh!
Are you ever going to make it to the ball?
Cinderella how you going to get your fella? Hey Hey!
When all you do is sit a crying in the hall.

While the story the same it's just words that have changed
(echo: words that have changed)

And the plot we've slightly (echo) rearranged
No more of the magic and Allakazam (echo: Allakazam)
Instead put your faith in God and trust in your fellow man
(echo: fellow man).

I once read an interesting book called "The Queen and I". It was a satirical novel about the royal family and I loved it. In the story, Princess Di sold Avon, Prince Charles grew hydroponic tomatoes, and the worst of all the corgis ran riot in the neighbourhood and interbred. I read this while I was recovering from my hysterectomy.

I found the whole hysterectomy thing was laughable, and decided to write a similar type of book which I called "Ursula and I", which was the name that I gave to my uterus. "Ursula" still features in my real story, but not actually as a satirical look at hysterectomies today, but as part of my life. It had caused me to question my existence, and my purpose for living. Friends who read it thought it was great and funny, so that fed my ego further to lead me to believe that I was indeed a writer (whatever that meant).

I knew I could tell a good story, and often did this when I was under the influence of 'bubbles', or a couple of gin and tonics. One of the things that I began to realise was that my storytelling and witting, as limited as it was, certainly became a way of me remembering things in my past. Importantly it was also a way of reminding me just how much of a part God played in my life, even though I didn't acknowledge it fully at times.

If you are reading this story, feeling as though everything in your life has let you down, and you are feeling a type of hopelessness and questioning as to whether God actually exists, I would encourage you to read on, and look back on the instances where you can see that, even though bad things happened to you, you are still here, just as I am today. Hopefully, by reflecting on this, it might just remind you that there is a purpose for your existence. God does exist and He loves you.

The book "Ursula" never really got finished, but much of her story is inside this one as it talks about my early years, and my journey with Jesus. Friends who knew me, and knew some things about my early years, marvelled at the way I had turned out, but they didn't know what was going on inside my head – and at what cost... People would say "How did you cope? And many would suggest that I should write my story for others to read, and that it would be helpful for them.

I guess looking back you could say that, despite the fact that my life was full of change and very different from other peoples, I cope, though previously I didn't realise exactly the part that Jesus played in keeping me safe, despite the circumstances that arose.

The crash came after my son died of an overdose of heroin, and circumstances after that lead to one calamity after another, until finally it all erupted into one catastrophic event. My demons were always hovering, even before this, as I tried to deal with one situation after another. But the event that led to the writing of this actually occurred after my son, Mark, died at 37.

Thank goodness for my husband, daughter, and good friends but, above all, to God my saviour whom, through all of this, held me up and kept me safe. He showed me I was purposed and loved, despite everything.

To you the reader, my story had changed. It is not about Ursula, it is not just a life about a little girl who grew up fighting for existence. This is a story about how, without her even knowing she was purposed and loved by

God, she was given people around to love, and for her to show them that they, too, were loved by God, and that God did, indeed, exist.

So, to you who are reading this book... look back on your life, and see just where God has shown you that He cares, even though you didn't know it then. You don't need to do anything, my friend. You just need to confirm that you believe in God, and that Jesus was the son of God who died for all our sins and who, through His grace by faith in the end, despite what happens in the world, we will have eternal life.

So, let's read on together…

Ironically, my story begins where my life could have ended, but it didn't, so maybe this story is part of my purpose. Not as a writer, but as someone who despite many unusual events in her life, came to know that God loved her and kept her safe.

As the famous poem, 'Footprints in the Sand' asks, "Why sometimes there was only one set of footprints in the sand?" And God replies, "That's because sometimes I needed to carry you", and He sure carried me, but I never got too heavy and He was always there.

So, come, if you have survived this far join me now as we begin the story and the day begins.

Chapter 1

——

Hangover guilt

As the day began, I opened my eyes and, similar to a computer, my brain started to formulate and process the night's events. My head ached, and I felt foggy, and the first recollections of what had happened began to emerge. I realized how dry my mouth was, and that I had a headache.

I squeezed my eyes tight, as if to try and block out any memory, but it wasn't happening. The computer brain was really firing up, and the memory of the fight, the yelling, the drama, and the falling over, came flooding in. This wasn't the first time this had happened. It had happened many times before, but with this one there was something that was different, and I couldn't quite work it out. Suddenly it hit me and, in a flashback to the night before, I saw my daughter's face. She was standing at the bottom of the bed, and my husband was standing with her, explaining that he was at his wits end, and didn't know what to do so he had to call her.

I saw her face quite clearly, and her voice as if it were just happening again at this very moment.

"So that's it is it?" she said. "You are prepared to just leave us all, Mum. Bailee and the kids. Nice, really nice, Mum!"

The revelation suddenly hit me. What had always been just a thought, a type of means of release from my depression and panic, had last night almost become a reality. I had taken a handful of pills that night in an effort to actually release myself from the current panic. I had taken the step, the step that I fantasized about as a relief from my pain, this time as a punishment for my husband and his perceived not caring, and ultimately a release from my torment That which I had only thought about doing on other occasions had now become an actual action.

My husband, in real time, appeared at the bottom of the bed, and I could see the look of concern on his face.

"Want a cuppa tea?" he asked.

"How are you feeling?"

I shook my head, and the tears starting streaming down my face as I lifted my arms for a cuddle.

"Why, Katie?" I asked. "Surely she didn't have to see this?"

"I was scared so scared," he replied. I just didn't know what else to do as I couldn't control you!"

He explained how I had ranted and raved, had fallen and lurched across a cupboard, and then I noticed the broken crystal vase on the floor. I understood now why I was aching on my left side. When I glanced in the mirror I could see congealed blood on the left-hand side of my face, and I grimaced and turned away. I remember now that I had fallen across the bed, and landed on the floor. Suddenly, so many of my actions came flooding forward in my memory.

I remember swallowing a number of tablets but then panicked, and stuck my fingers down my throat. As I don't have many tablets, the only things I had were some antihistamines. My husband had phoned the 'Nurse on Call' number, who suggested that I go to causality. But I had refused.

It was just too complicated and frightening at this early stage in the morning. To examine, in detail, what had caused this desperate reaction, and particularly the anger, but undoubtedly alcohol had played a major part. Compared to the week before, that day had been wonderful. Friends had come around, and I had been drinking with them outside on the deck in the Sun and, of course, had not eaten. They were Keith's friends, and it was nice to just be myself in front of them, rather than 'Mrs Principal' as I am perceived by many of his mates. Socially I can be quite funny when I have had a few drinks and, indeed, the 'life of the party', which makes Keith cross.

Leading up to this day, the week before had been bad. My son had once again gone off the rails with his drug problem and I couldn't find him. I had also had an argument at the golf club, and therefore felt very vulnerable. For some unknown reason that week, my best friend and I had parted ways or, at least, I had withdrawn and I thought I just didn't care.

I had had enough of everyone telling me how good they were, and how wonderful their families were. After a couple of bottles of wine I felt on top of the world, confident and assured of the fact that I was intelligent and well liked, only to crash through the wall that evening. I was sick of the voices in my head telling me that I was useless, ugly, and that everyone hated me. That afternoon I was mixing in with Keith friends, and becoming the life of the party, I felt good. The voices were wrong, and I was a star who had found new friends. I had had enough of being Mrs Principal, being socially correct, and certainly had enough alcohol to feel untouchable... So what had happened?

I looked up at Keith and then I realised. We had had a terrible argument. He had said how ashamed he was about how I had acted. I was swearing and telling fairly risqué jokes, etc and then, despite his subtle warnings, I kept ridiculing him in front of his friends.

I remember swinging at him, and screaming at him, accusing him of things that had happened in the past, and blaming him for the way my son was acting.

The more he tried to console me and hold me, the more I thrashed around throwing whatever I could find at him. In real time, I glanced up and was relieved that there were at least no marks on his face.

I had had enough, and somehow this all had to be over. I knew the only way this was to be over was if I took control myself. I had acted out, in my head this scenario many times before, as a release from other episodes where I was out of control. The way for this to end, and me not to face any repercussion, was to end it all. I had had enough. I remembered feeling exhausted as I reached for the tablets that I had on my bedside table. I remember also praying aloud to myself and asking God to please meet me, and let me into Heaven, even though I knew that what I doing was a sin. For some reason I never considered suicide as a mortal sin, but believed that God would understand, considering what a horrible life and what a mixed-up person I was. Yet I loved Him, and acknowledged him as my saviour.

The next bit is a bit confusing but, slowly and surely, the memory of my actions that night became crystal clear.

My husband had grabbed the bottle, and then started screaming at me.

"How many have you taken?" he bellowed. I didn't know exactly how many, and they were only antihistamines. He ran out of the room, and I heard him yelling into the phone: "Send an ambulance!"

As I said earlier, this part is a bit confusing, I can't remember clearly what happened exactly, as by now I was drifting in and out of a kind of drunken slumber. He kept banging my back, and telling me to put my fingers down my throat and to try and be sick. The ambulance arrived and they started to examine me, asking questions of both my husband and I.

It seems that I wasn't in any mortal danger, but needed to be watched for other signs. They were going to take me to hospital, but I started to get very upset so it was decided that, as Keith was there and Kate was staying, I could stay home, but would be expected to visit my GP in the morning.

They all walked out. I slept! And so back to the beginning…

That's what happened! But I knew this time it wasn't just going to end after a few days. I had to do something about this. The actual action of the attempt had gone beyond anything before, and it even scared me, despite the fact that it was a pretty stupid and unplanned thing to do.

I started in my usual way to plan my own recovery. OK, I would go to my doctor and, maybe, I could blame the new pills she had given me to help me relax and sleep… Yes, that's a good one I thought… It's not really my fault. I could ring each of Keith's friends and apologise, and have them back for dinner… But I knew that this time there was no way I could take control of the situation. Tears rolled down my face, and all I could do was recite my prayer and hope… *"Gentle Jesus, meek and mild, look upon a little child; pity my simplicity, and suffer me to come to Thee."* **Please, God. Help me! I don't want to die!!!**

My regular doctor for 30 years had left, but I decided to stay at the clinic with a new doctor. I had discussed with her the fact that I wasn't sleeping well, and so she changed my medication. I had noticed, prior to this, that at times I was a little angry, but I was sleeping better. My husband told me that my doctor had rung, and wanted to see me that day. I think this happened because of ringing the 'Nurse on Call', and I suspect that she had notified my doctor of my miserable attempt at suicide.

My visit was not something that I neither wanted, nor was ready to do, given my current state of anxiety. As I sat in the surgery, I felt totally hopeless and vulnerable. As I entered her rooms, I am not sure what happened, or what her question was, but I just started howling and babbling about my life, my feelings, etc, and how I just didn't want to go on anymore. I was quite stunned when she seemed to know a lot about my life, and she explained how I had issues of abandonment. Her recommendation was that I see a clinical psychologist and, agreeing to this, an appointment was made for the following week.

While I agreed to go, by the time the appointment came around I was not happy at all. I had been to see people before and My visit was not something that I either wanted or was ready to do given my current state of anxiety, although they were trying to be helpful, I just felt that they never understood me.

Usually I was sent to someone in order to deal with a major event in my life that had caused me to panic. Generally these events were associated with school, or my son, and they had a limited time span. These visits involved strategies to help me get over the particular issue.

As an example of this, and perhaps to show readers just how over the top I can become, one such issue involved sunburn at my school. As part of the Christmas celebrations, the kids were to have a carol's service outside with each grade singing a carol. I had checked the weather, which was to be 23 degrees. It was a great afternoon, and many parents came. We provided seats for the parents, and each child was made to wear a hat and sunscreen. They were also provided with a cool drink from McDonalds. If a child did not have a hat then we provided one made from paper.

The next day, three parents came to the office complaining about their children getting sunburn on the knee. One in particular was very angry, and was threatening legal action. She was taking her child to the doctor.

I was understanding, but explained all the precautions we had taken. Despite the explanation, they were still very unhappy. That night it was the school concert and, after the concert, we only had one day to go till breakup day.

That night I went into panic mode. The next morning I got a list of all the kids who were not at the concert, and also not a school the next day. There were about 150 in total. I set about phoning each parent subtly, trying to find out if they were suffering from the Sun.

Breaking up that day, I had about six parents that I needed to ring before Christmas, as I had not been able to contact them. I left the Christmas school staff party early and went back to school to keep ringing, not that any of the staff knew where I was going. At some stage my daughter, and the school psychiatrist, came and found me walking in circles refusing to go home. I am not sure how or why they actually came looking for me. They took me to the doctor, where I was injected with Valium, and I was told that I would need to attend the surgery the next day.

I had three subsequent appointments with a clinical psychologist, and each day I got better. In the end I couldn't believe how I had over-reacted. As he pointed out, no one would have gone to the lengths that we did to protect kids, with hats, sunscreen, drinks, etc. I guess the big question was: wouldn't they all be outside at lunch anyway? The one parent, who was very angry, also rang me to say that her child had worms which, undoubtedly, she had caught from our toilets! She was quite weird really, and I knew this, yet I let her have this power over me, believing that I was in the wrong and she could destroy me.

I should try and explain also that, when I am in this state, my mind goes in many negative directions. In the case of the sunburn issue, I felt I was already in court. That the judge had found me guilty, I was stripped of everything, and put into gaol. Writing this, even now, it seems so silly, but that is when I was in the worst possible place, I knew things couldn't get worse, and so anything that happened after that could not affect me. It's kind of like experiencing, and living through, the worst possible scenario so that the real solution isn't really that bad because I have already coped with the worst.

The short-term support and help usually needs to only last for a couple of weeks, or until the issue is resolved, and then I just sit and panic about when the next one will be, and wondering if the next will be the one that breaks me forever.

That's the pattern that has been part of my adult life ever since I can remember. The example I used was sunburn, but there have been far too many instances like this for me to explain them all. This current outburst, however, that forced me to finally sit down and write, was different. It didn't fit my usual pattern, and the result in attempting suicide made it even scarier.

Chapter 2

Meeting Sarah

However, this time I don't believe there was a single issue, but a compilation of many things happening around me. I knew that my time with this psychologist would not be short-term if I really wanted to understand, and deal with, these behaviours.

I was probably laying the blame for my episode on the medication that my new GP had prescribed, but she wasn't having bar of this, and was insisting that I needed ongoing support. The GP actually rang the psychiatrist and made the appointment for me, as she claimed that this particular person would be busy, and may not be taking new patients. I got the appointment, and it was the next week! Sometimes I think that doctors have a secret code amongst themselves that they can wangle appointments, etc, when they believe that it is important.

When I entered her rooms, and she introduced herself, I certainly gave out the message that I was there under sufferance, and that I really didn't think this would be helpful. I told her, in no uncertain terms, that this would not be of any use, and that I was now quite OK.

"That's okay," she said. "Let's just start and see where it leads."

I am still unsure how it started, or what questions she asked, but suddenly tears were flowing, and stuff was coming out of my mouth about my life as a child and adolescent. Her suggestion was that I try and write the events that I was talking about into a timeline, so they were ordered and made logical sense.

The answers as to why, at 68, I was suddenly suffering such sever panic and anxiety attacks, which now had led me to a possible suicide attempt, seemed to lie in my past. Sarah, the psychiatrist, thought that perhaps, if I isolated and examined these events and arranged them in some sort of chronological order, then I may be able to cope with the fear and panic more readily by identifying the source.

In the very short time that we had been together she had pointed out that, as a child, I had really missed out on things, like parenting, and that my life as a child was not normal.

Somehow she seemed to be telling me that, from where she sat, it was amazing that I turned out as I did, given the circumstances that I had been through. She said, to her, it wasn't surprising at all that I sometimes reacted the way that I did.

This was the second time in my life that someone had actually told me they thought I was incredible and, while I heard what she said, I really couldn't believe it. Just as I couldn't believe the first time when someone had told me that I was beautiful, stunning, and had incredibly long legs. I had always found compliments of any kind difficult to believe.

The question was where to begin. I had always questioned why I was born. What real purpose did I have in this life? As the years go past, and age sets in, there are many additions and repairs that need to happen to the female human body in order to keep it. I had always felt flawed, as though I never really belonged in the world, and that the world would have been better off without me. I wondered if this thought stemmed from not being able to have children. I never talked about this much to anyone any more, but perhaps it was a major cause of my self-destruction. Could this be the missing link, the catalyst for these attacks?

Not being able to have children through an ovarian deficiency, which was finally diagnosed at the age of 17, had certainly made me feel different. But I felt I had gotten over it, and somehow managed to wing my way through puberty. The saving grace was "Ursula", my womb. I had a womb and, with hormone treatment, periods started and all felt somewhat normal. I don't think that anyone really understood the change that happened when I had the hysterectomy.

Having the hysterectomy at 45 was something that really had an impact on me, yet I said nothing to anyone. I treated it as a joke, and three times cancelled the appointment on the pretences that I had other things on. Finally the gynaecologist got so angry that his receptionist rang the school, and spoke to my secretary. I couldn't escape anymore, as 'the dragon' (secretary, and now best friend) had it under her control.

It's funny looking back how this event actually came out of a panic situation. I had gained the principal position at the school and, to my memory, this was the first appointment, in a primary school, to the principal class in Geelong under Merit and Equity.

It was expected that the incumbent, who had been running the school, would get the job. The weird thing was when the school council president knocked on my door to tell me that I had been successful. There stood a clown! Naturally I thought this was some kind of cruel joke, but it wasn't, it was real. He was the actual school council president, whose afternoon job was as a clown.

In my case you could bet that, with this success, something would go wrong, and it did. The boys were not happy, and the union was equally not happy. An appeal occurred from the incumbent, something which was unheard of, as appeals can only be done before the process.

I went through hell! Constantly wondering what the appeal would be about, as you are not permitted to know. What part of the process was wrong? (Could it be the clown?) To make matters worse, my best friend, whom I loved, put an ad in the Geelong Advertiser congratulating me on the appointment as the first elected primary principal in Geelong, not understanding about the appeal process. As all principals in the primary division were male, so you can imagine how this went down amongst 'the boys'. The wait time for the appeal was unbelievable. Just not knowing, and not being able to fix it, had a huge impact on me.

Gossip was everywhere regarding what the appeal was about and, unfortunately, no one other than the appellant, and the union, had any knowledge. During this waiting period, as part of my panic, I was hospitalized and sedated. I saw a psychologist whilst in hospital and, as part of telling him my history regarding a lack of oestrogen, he ordered bone density tests.

Perhaps one of the most hideous of disease, that women have to deal with, is osteoporosis. I acknowledge that it does affect men also, but it seems that women are statistically more affected. There are a number of causes that leave people susceptible to this debilitating process, one of which it is believed that a lack of estrogens.

For me, at the ripe old age of 45, this became an important revelation. Childless through a lack of estrogens in my productive years, had led to concern by doctors as to the state of my bones. This evidence, coupled with the fact that absorption powers for vitamin D was minimal, led to me having a nuclear scan. It was no surprise to anyone that these results were devastating. I didn't even manage to make the grid. At this rate, I would have a dowager hump, ribs removed, etc, by the time I was 60.

Luckily I was sent to the top person in the field. Having sustained two back fractures already, I was to be given oestrogen on a regular basis. Also, if I agreed, a medication called Fossmax as well, to be taken daily to assist with the prevention of fractures.

All in all, I didn't really think that this was such a bad thing, until the diagnosis went further and mentioned that it would be appropriate for me to have a full hysterectomy, given that I was taking oestrogen.

No one seemed to understand just how important it was, for me, to maintain what was left of my female 'bits', especially since they hadn't really produced anything worthwhile except a few periods, and maybe one possible conception.

The appointment was made, and that was that. I would be entering hospital to be removed of my bits, and my bones would benefit. There was no question that this was the right thing. No one really asked how I felt. Many women had this operation. After all, why would I need these special bits? This was the general thought pattern between my doctor and the family. No one, I don't think, really asked me how I felt. It was just going to be done in order to keep me from possible cancer, caused through the continuation of progesterone and oestrogen.

I remember lying on the bed that night before the operation, thinking about what this would mean, and my hand reached down to caress my vagina and then slowly upward to where I supposed my uterus would be. A tear formed in my eye, and a feeling of hopelessness and loss crept over me.

"I am sorry, Ursula," I whispered. "We have been through a lot together, and I am glad you were there. I really am, even though we didn't have a baby in there."

I hate hospitals, doctors, nurses, etc, and the process of being in hospital scares me because I felt like I was out of control. I think it stems from the days that I watched my father die, and watched the hospital do nothing.

My dad died at the ripe old age of 38. He died of a massive cerebral haemorrhage and, ironically, it was on the first Saturday that Polly Farmer played football for Geelong.

I got to live with father for about 12 months, and he built me a house. Life was wonderful when this happened. I was playing netball, and went across to Kardinia Park to watch the final quarter of the Geelong game, little knowing that it was my father that they carried around the outside of the oval. I visited him each lunchtime time in hospital, coming from school at lunchtime, trying to feed him. When he was initially admitted, he could write because he was left-handed but could not speak, and his face was twisted down the right-hand side. On the first visit he wrote telling me not to let people see him like he was. He was a very proud man, who took great pride in his appearance.

On the final day, I stood watching the air pump go in and out until finally it stopped. Doctors were around, but they kept calling for his doctor and announcing 'code red'. Finally his doctor came after he died, and I saw red. I hit him and tried to kick him. I was subdued, given a needle, and put in a hospital bed. Nan and Uncle Phil came, and got me the next day. I was never charged, but was supposed to go see some physiatrist, which I never did. This whole experience with dad really set a lifetime hatred of hospitals for me. The experience I had as a child with my father and hospitals, was burnt into my memory. They were bad places, where no-one cared.

Ironically, the day I was booked in to go to hospital, started off badly. My husband and I walked into Admission. I was hopeful that, as a private patient, I would get to be in the new part, the Birdseye Wing, but that wasn't to be! In reception I was given a brown paper bag with my history in it. I couldn't believe it. My life was nothing more than a brown paper bag. A nurse came over, and gave me a present from my friend, Tom. Inside was a bigger brown paper bag, and a note that said, "Put this over your head, Dragon, so they don't have to look at you!" It was, of course, sent with love.

The real irony of the actual day came when a little old lady, with a huge dowager hump, came to take me to the ward. Here am I going to have this operation to avoid this 'hump' and, what do I get? Right in my face!

"Walk this way," she said, as she limped across the room. My husband was standing there and, for one full second, I was tempted to copy her walk, dowager hump and all. But I saw his face, and knew that he knew exactly what I was going to do, so I didn't

Along the passage we went, until we came to 'The House of Death'. This is the old Kardinia ward. I had been there when my father died, and could still remember the stale, sickly smell. I am shown to a three-bed ward, with a man and an old lady (hooked up to tubes and machines) already occupying the room.

"Your bed's here love," my little dowager humped volunteer says, as she points to the middle bed.

My husband goes to put my things on the bed, but I grab his arm.

"Not going there!" I announce, and leave the room.

After a short discussion, led by me announcing that I was not going to stay there, as that is where my father died. By this time a nursing sister had arrived, and said that I can't change my mind. The theatre has been booked, as has this room, and nothing can be changed.

"Not my problem," I replied.

I continued to walk along the passage towards the exit. After following me along the corridor, yapping about how this is not normal, etc, and getting nowhere, I am told to sit down. A discussion takes place outside of the waiting room. I can still see the plastic flowers, and the fridge which was there when dad died, and his death appears in my conscious mind. I am shaking with fear.

After a few phone calls, and mutterings in the office, the boss lady appears, and I am told to follow the nurse along the passage. Finally we come to the newly constructed Birdsey Wing, and I am happy. I settle on the bed, then in comes the head honcho.

Obviously she has been prepared for the likes of me by her predecessor. She introduces herself, and then explains what will happen tomorrow. About how important it is for me to go to the toilet as soon after the operation as I can, in order to get home quickly.

She then asked, "What is your agenda for your stay here, Nola?"

I look her squarely in the eye and answered. "To get out of this shit hole as quickly as possible."

"Good," came the reply. "Because mine is to get rid of assholes like you as soon as we can, so we should get on well!"

We hit it off immediately.

When I was in pain after the operation, she was marvellous. So caring and helpful. She arranged for me to have portable pain-relief machine that I could control so that I could get home quickly. I spent two days in there, and was packed and ready to depart on the third day at 7.00am, much to the disgust of the lady over the road from me who was in there for four days already, and was trying to stay in for another two.

"Why are you doing this?" she said to me in anger. "You are making it so hard for the rest of us."

"Why?" I asked.

"Well," she replied, "I have four kids at home, and I want to stay here for as long as I can. But you you're up and running around as if nothing has happened."

The hysterectomy story could go on, but I will cut it short. My recovery was almost non-existent. The very old male gynaecologist insisted that I do nothing, lift nothing, don't drive, etc. I did all of these, and went back to school after two weeks. Something needs to be updated for hysterectomies, as they need to understand that we don't drive trucks, we have power steering in our cars, washing machines, driers, etc, so I reckon we can do lots of things.

And stitches are dissolvable nowadays!

No doubt in my own mind the hysterectomy had an effect on me. For a while I felt somewhat lost, different, but things soon settled down. I realised that this panic, caused by the appeal, was good thing in a way. The appeal itself was unheard of in previous appointments, because it can only be lodged by something being wrong with the process. To my knowledge, that had never happened in Geelong before.

In my case the union had felt that the process had been polluted because I had only been in the principal class for two years, and I had to be there three years before I could apply. However, they were wrong, and the appeal was not upheld because the government had eliminated Support Centres, so my previous principal appointment was no longer valid.

However, this process took about three months, and I lived in limbo not knowing what was going on. I was feeling very unsure as I was not permitted to ask anything regarding the procedure. I finished up in hospital with what was a type of breakdown. Often we can't see the hand of God in things, as this turned out to be a good thing. It identified my osteoporosis, caused through a lack of oestrogen, and it would allow me to get early treatment. While these were factors in my life, they were things that could happen to anyone and were not necessarily the things that caused my depression and anxiety. I needed to go way back, as Sarah suggested, if I was to find the cause of my panics and fear. I also I needed to arrange things, from my early life, in some sort of chronological order.

I wasn't too sure how I would do this, as I had started writing many things about my life, but everything was jumbled and then left for months without any correction. Subsequently I lost interest.

As Sarah suggested, somehow the answer lay in the past and, even though I knew it would be painful, I needed to go there and try and make sense of everything.

I was scared, as I knew there were some things in my early life that I refused to let myself think about, but felt that now this needed to be done.

The one consolation I had was that Sarah would remain with me for my journey to the past, even though my 12 free sessions had elapsed. In my own mind, I wondered just how far back I should go. I could remember certain things from about three onwards, and some things from the past I had been told by relatives and people who knew my family background, but I wondered just how reliable my memory would be. How do I work out the truth?

For instance, I am petrified of lions. I can't watch jungle movies, like Tarzan, or whenever I go to the zoo I can't go anywhere near lions. My mother told me that, when I was really little, she took me to the zoo and I saw a little girl put her hand in the lion cage to pat the lion. He pulled her in and ripped her arm up, and there was lots of blood. Apparently I would scream if I went down past the town hall, where the two concrete lion statutes sat, and I would just scream and refuse to walk past. I don't remember the little girl, but I still am petrified of lions and could never go to Africa because of the lions! Neither will I walk past the town hall, but I will go around. See my dilemma? You be the judge? And judge my early stories for yourself.

Chapter 3

Some of my Background

So much I had put out of my mind about my early childhood and, as life had turned out, there seemed to be no point in remembering any of it. Often I would try to say something, but my husband would say: "No need to talk about that as it is in the past, and you have me now."

Over the many years I had developed many scenarios for different friends, which protected me from being hurt and could, I believed, make me vulnerable. Some of these explained why parents weren't around, or I would make up stories as to where I had been previously in my life. What was sometimes difficult, in later years, was to remember which of the scenarios were appropriate for my audience. Quite often though, a weakness would appear and I would forget what I had said.

When this happened, it gave my demons a chance to attack. "Ha! Ha!" they would taunt me. "See now you are in trouble. You are a liar, and people now know you are dumb and stupid, and you have something to hide."

When I believed I was caught out, I would panic and think that this would mean that people knew how broken I was. As a consequence, they wouldn't play with me. I needed so much to be liked by everyone. I just couldn't cope when this happened.

Why did this happen? I wanted to know, and Sarah suggested that I needed to look at my childhood. So here we go. The real story begins…

I was born on the 9th of March in 1947, a post-war baby and, according to my mother (who claims at times that I was not the child that she delivered, but rather the one that had been thrust upon her), I was indeed a horror. She described my hair as though a lawn mower had run over it, and told me that I screamed morning to night. I don't have any baby photos, or any photos at all except one when I was about two. I looked OK, a little boofy, perhaps, but really quite cute.

My mother was a schizophrenic, diagnosed at the age of 22. Of course, in those days, it was not referred to as, this but rather as a type of madness. I am sure they wanted a baby but, as both parents expressed, not this particular one. My father was desperate for a boy and, according to mum, never spoke, held, or touched me till I was about two.

Mum wanted a dark-skin brown-eyed baby that looked like her, not a pale-skinned screaming angry child with reddish-yellow hair. My grandmother was an important character in my life from birth to about five years of age. She is actually recorded on my birth certificate as the person registering the birth, and is also listed as present at my birth. I can remember her teaching me about God and Jesus and, even then, I had a very simplistic faith that this God was in charge of everything, and that He loved me and would look after me.

Most of the times I still have this belief but, when my demons arise, I am thrown in turmoil, and question where God is, and what He is like. I question why, if He is real, does He let this stuff happen to me. But eventually, each time up till now, I can look back and know that He is there and with me, even in the bad times. He has to be because, in reality, I would not have survived.

During these times of panic and anxiety, my faith is questioned and, to me, that is the scary part, because I can no longer protect myself against the unknown which can gobble me up and spit me out. Leaving me, like He did Job, sitting in the gutter.

However, unlike Job, I sometimes believe that I don't have the faith to go on, and I need to find my own strength when under attack from my demons. What scares me is that I have the power, and knowledge, on how to overcome my panic, fear, anxiety, and depression through suicide, something I have contemplated at times and, indeed, something that has made me seek help from a clinical psychologist, and follow a different strategy to hopefully gain some normality. A strategy that, through prayer and understanding, is more about the nature of my God, and my beautiful Jesus, that He will never leave us and He is faithful. ***Deuteronomy 31.6 says that He will continually bless us, just as he did JOB.***

I guess it all began in 1947, the year of my birth, and much of what I can recall was information I was given from parents, grandparents, friends, and relatives.

However, some things I can recall as clear as if it was yesterday, and some I am a bit unsure of… Evidence exists now of prenatal factors having a big influence on the foetus and so, to get the real picture, we need to go back before 1947.

My grandmother, on my mother's side, did not want them to marry. My mother was not yet 18 and she had the power to stop this wedding. My father's mother also didn't want them to marry, claiming that my dad had been away some four years in the war. She could not stop them, and often blamed my nana for not using her power to stop it. They were married about two months after Dad came home from the war in 1945.

They had been childhood sweethearts since the age of 15 and, at Mum's eulogy, I had the great pleasure of retelling the many stories she had told me about their courtship.

As a young couple they had it all. They built a house in Hector Street, and all the family, including my uncle, pitched in to help. My mother was working at the woollen mills prior to her marriage and, apparently with Dad away, learnt to drink, smoke and, in general, have a good time. She continued to live this life while my father, on his return from the army, considered himself above this and hated her working, as none of his friend's wives did.

Most of my father's friends were wealthy and, I think, to some degree, Dad imagined he was also. He had very different standards and morals. Mum was no longer the doting sweetheart that he had romanced and left behind four years before, but a woman of the world. Dad considered Mum's friends lower class, and smoking (which Mum did incessantly) absolutely disgusting!

I am not sure about the truth of this, but Mum said that every second weekend my dad, and his two friends, would go to Aireys Inlet where they were able to get alcohol after 6.00pm. They would, stay the night with three ladies, and then come home on a Sunday to commence life in suburbia. How true, I don't really know, but I do have a picture of a car my dad had, that ended up over a cliff and, except for a tree, would have killed them all. This occurred on the way home from Aireys Inlet.

I got to know many of Dad's friends as 'uncles', and their wives as 'aunties'. That was the life and family situation that I was born into. I never got to know many of Mum's friends at all, as they were never constant.

Having been married for two years, I guess it was expected that they should have a baby, so I am pretty sure I was planned. But for what reasons each wanted a child, other than to confirm to the norm, we will never know.

I can look back now, from the outside, and I want to scream at them" "Don't do it! Split up!" I say this, not out of anger but rather out of love.

Recently my friends and I were talking about National Service (Vietnam) and three of my friends had husbands in the draft. Each agreed how changed their husbands were when they came home from the war, and how devastating the war was. I see my dad, a strapping 18-year-old, in love with the girl down the road and with a possible football career in the AFL.

Suddenly he is conscripted into army and sent to New Guinea, where he was one of the longest serving soldiers. He caught Malaria and. although he never chose to talk much about life over there, he was always full of praise for his New Guinea Guide (Po Po).

As a munition's driver, I know he lost four sentry guards from his truck, and he also fought in hand-to-hand combat against two Japanese soldiers, in a tent. Four years of his life, then home to find his girlfriend a mature woman of the world, working, independent, smoking, drinking, going into pubs, and often talking to herself. How could this marriage possibly work?

Sometimes, being able to be retrospective is great. Isn't it?

Chapter 4

The Early Years 0-5 (as Sarah Suggested)

My life was weird but, to me, it was normal. With my parents constantly in conflict with each other, and alcohol playing a large part, life for me was unpredictable. I can't remember ever being held or cuddled, except from my nanas. For me, as a child, this was the norm, and I knew no other life.

The one thing that I did have, was two sets of grandparents who cared about me, and loved me. In a sense, they became my only parents as Mum and Dad would constantly leave me with them when they went out, split-up, or fought. In my early years my father's parents, were predominately the grandparents I was sent to as they lived in Geelong, but Nan and Pop Tompkins (Mum's side) were always part of my life and, after "The Big Split", they became really prominent.

I can recall the wicker chair and cot in my bedroom at Hector Street, even though I was only three. This was the place that I would be either commanded to go to, or else was placed unceremoniously there. My father would continually yell at me to stop crying, and would shut the door. It is funny the things you remember. For me, a fight was always accompanied by the gramophone playing "Irene Goodnight", a song that my father hated, and I learnt to recognize as a warning. One thing that my mother did was to teach me songs and poems at a very early age.

She would make me do the actions to the songs as well. My grandfather used to call me "Chatty" short for chatterbox, as I was always talking. Mum told me that I spoke in sentences at the age of nine months, but I have my doubts. She also gloated that I was potty-trained at nine months!!!

It would be wrong to say that my life was cruel one, but some of my memories aren't all that clear. Kids today are often told to sit in the "naughty corner" but when the fights started, I could be thrown into the wicker cot in my room. If I dared cry I would get slapped, mostly by my father. Sometimes this would happen during the day when he would call in whilst driving the truck, and find my mother still in bed or, worse, still drunk and delusional.

I never really knew when these day fights would happen but, if I heard the record any night, I would run to my room by myself and climb in, and hide under the blankets. The record was always played when they were fighting at night. I had a blue wicker chair next to the cot that I could stand on and get over the sides. For many years after this, I had a disease on my fingers that the doctors said was from a "wicker germ". I still have flare-ups on my fingers today.

I didn't have any young friends, and my parents never really associated with people who had four-year-old children, or at least Dad didn't. So how was I supposed to know what was, and was not, responsible parenting. I guess that, after you become a parent yourself, the responsibilities and roles of parenting become more clearly defined, although I am not claiming brilliance in this area.

We never went anywhere, as a family, except to my grandparent's houses. Dad never took me anywhere, but some afternoons Mum would take me to the pub with her. Even at this age, I can remember the rules quite clearly. I would be made to perform, but would never be allowed to accept a soft drink, or chips and stuff, from any of her men friends. Once a man tried to make me sit on his knee, but my mother grabbed me, pulled me off, belted me, and then proceeded to belt into him. We were thrown out of the pub, but it didn't take her long to find another, any pub would do except 'The White Heart', which was where my father drank.

I knew not to go there, even though I knew where it was, because one afternoon, while Mum was drinking, she told me to go and look in the shops for a while. When I came back, she wasn't in the pub, and a man I knew said that she had gone. I panicked, and raced up Moorabool Street to the White Heart Hotel to tell Dad, and to hopefully get home some way. My aunty owned the pub, took me into the kitchen, gave me lemonade, and called my father.

I knew, as soon as he looked at me, that I was in trouble. "Look what I found wandering in the lounge," she said to Dad. "Seems she can't find Jean."

My dad grabbed my arm, and pulled me out of the kitchen into the street. "Don't you ever come in here again," he bellowed. "Never! You understand!"

"Get the bus, and get home to Ocean Grove, and I'll see you tonight," he roared, thrusting a ten pound note into my hand. There I stood, in Moorabool Street, with ten quid to get myself home. Dad was always throwing money at me, as though that would make things right.

Even though I was only about five, I knew how to catch the bus. But the worst thing was waiting, after I got home, to see if either of them would actually come home. The last bus was at 11.30 and, if neither was home by then, I would have to decide whether I would go to Nan and Pop's, which was about two kilometres away.

This was not such a good thing because I didn't really like the dark, and I would have to make a decision as to whether I took a short cut through the Methodist church grounds (really freaky at night), or go the long way. Usually I just closed my eyes, prayed my prayer, "Gentle Jesus, meek and mild" …and then ran through the church grounds as hard as I could.

For a few months we all stayed together in a little flat in Ocean Grove this waiting was a regular occurrence and I suppose I just got used to it. If I had run to Nana and Pops then I would stay there the Sunday as well so that was okay. Often I stayed longer until in the end I just stayed at Nan and Pops and went to school from there until I was taken back to Geelong to my other nana's.

The last time this happened would be a day I would never forget, and a day that I have never talked about before. Dad picked me up, and we had to pick up Mum. She was at a picnic for Waterside Workers at Eastern Beach, with my aunty. As we arrived Mum came over to the car, she was pretty drunk. She wanted Dad and I to stay, but Dad said he wouldn't stay with that "scum".

He told her to get in the car, as he wouldn't be coming back. Reluctantly she got in. Dad drove a Mercury, which had an arm rest in the back seat, and I used to sit on this and pretend that I was the queen, and wave to people. They started yelling, and then fighting. We were driving along Ormond Road and, in those days, there were tram tracks down the middle, and big elm trees on the side of the road.

Dad was hitting her, and then Mum hit him and the car swerved. We hit a tree, and the impact caused Dad's door to fly open. The door hit a man on a bike, and he fell onto the tracks. He died! Police, ambulance, and people, were everywhere. Dad told me to stay in the car, and say nothing to anybody, but I heard what he said to Mum. He told her to say she was driving at the time, and not him, as he was a truck driver. He would lose his licence, and we would have no money. I am pretty sure Mum did this, as nothing happened, and I heard Dad say to the policeman that I was asleep on the back seat, so would not know anything. No one asked me anything about the accident.

While this story happened when I was about five, looking back I could see that things weren't right. Who would send their four-year-old child some two kilometres to the shops, across very busy roads, to get a piece of pumpkin? Who would refuse to get out of bed in the mornings and feed the child, and demand that the child bring in food to her while she chatted away to her "voices"? Who would insist that she hide when her father came home, because she said he was going to kill us with a knife if he was in a bad mood? On the other hand, who would teach her how to cook, read her stories, dance with her, knit the most beautiful jumpers and, at another time, abuse and slap her for being spoilt?

Yes, that was my life, and perhaps too that's where my demons, ie panic and obsession, had their beginnings. These demons that now, at 68, rear their heads frequently, and send me into a black hole of depression with feelings of unworthiness.

I can remember my life became one of entertaining myself. I taught my dolls schoolwork, and I parented them as I knew parenting, slapping them when they were naughty. I lived in a world of make-believe. Reality came with my grandparents on my father's side. Here I was loved and, when the night tremors came, my nana and pa would take me to their bed, cuddle me, feed me with chocolates, and sing me to sleep. My dream was always the same ... *"Blind dingoes were chasing me up a lamppost, and I had to jump off into the sea if I was to survive. I would fall, and fall, but would always wake up before I hit the water."*

That's one for you to ponder and work out. Weird, eh!

At their house I was never alone, they would always come. I don't have any real evidence but, in my own house, I have a feeling of sometimes crying and screaming for hours, and knowing that no one was coming. Even now my husband tells me that I sometimes get the "Moo Moos", as he calls them, and I yell out incoherently into the night.

My grandparents fascinated me, and I would often catch them kissing and cuddling each other, something that I had never seen my parents do.

I can't remember the number of times my parents would physically hit each other, split up, and then get back together. It seemed that Mum would always leave, and Dad would be home with me, but only long enough to pack me off to Nanas. I lost count of the number of times that my parents actually split up, and then came back together. Sometimes I would wake up in the morning looking for them, and Dad would say that she had gone, and that we were going to Nanas. I never really asked "gone where?" I was just relieved that I would go to Nanas, and life would be okay. I got to recognize the signs, and could prepare myself for the change that was about to happen. In this way it didn't seem to hurt as much.

One big fight came when I was four, and we were still living in Hector Street. It was big, and one I remember vividly, as I went with Mum for the first time. My dad came home quite late, and Mum had been sipping sherry. She was dressed up in her black and white dress (another indication of trouble) and announced that she was going out and, that "if it was good enough for the goose then it was good enough for the gander". I can recall those exact words as she used to make me say the poem 'Goosey, goosey, gander, where do you wander?'

My mother called a taxi, and my dad tried to stop her going out the front door. Finally he swung her around, and pushed her over the porch in the front of the house, just as the taxi came. Mum ran back inside to get me, but my father had grabbed me. I started screaming for Mum.

"You want her, well you have her, because you'll probably end up just like she is," my dad yelled, and over the porch I went also. We drove away in the night to a strange house, where a strange man helped my mother out of the taxi. Somehow I knew that this was to be the beginning of the end, and I would never see our Hector Street house again.

This time, the pattern had changed. I wasn't going to Nanas, my mum said we were going to a man's place, and that he would be like a father to me. We would be a family. This had never happened before, and I felt weird about it, but my mum was there so maybe it would be okay.

It was apparent from the start that the man had not expected me, and I could hear my mother assuring him that I was a good kid, and would cause no problems as I always amused myself. I saw his eyes glare at me and I knew that, no matter what I did, I would not be welcome there. But I never imagined the lengths he would go to actually get rid of me.

He had a motor bike with a sidecar, and one morning he insisted that I travel in the sidecar, with my mother on the pillion seat (my previous position). Half way down the hill the sidecar flew off, and it crashed into the side of the road. Nothing serious for me though, cuts and bruises, and a day later diagnosed with a broken wrist. Not long after that, when we were fishing in his boat, I hooked a flathead, even with my arm broken and in plaster but, on the way up, a shark took the flathead. I tried to pull on the hand line, but burnt my fingers as I wouldn't let go.

"Let her do it," he cried. "She can do it."

By this time I was almost half way out of the boat. My mother cut the line, and I fell back. She glared at him, and told him in no uncertain terms to take us back to shore. I heard only a part of their conversation, but my mother assured him that, if for any reason I should find myself overboard, she would dive in and save me, not him, and I think that was the last straw.

Everyone knew that my mother was an excellent swimmer, and I don't even think he could swim.

When we arrived back, a taxi was called. He went out and Mum and I drove in the taxi to my Nana Read's house. Hooray! Home at last, and no longer would I have to sleep on the floor in that horrible old room, and have the smell of salt in my nostrils.

It was decided that we would stay there together. Dad, Mum and I. Hector Street had been sold by Mum, and Dad had agreed to try again. So in the interim, Nana's house would be home. I was beside myself. They could fight all they liked; I would have my nana and my friends, Billy and Rhonda from next door, to play with.

Unfortunately the peace did not last! My uncle and his wife had moved in also, and Mum and my aunt did not get along. When you think of it, there were three married women all living in the same house.

I have been asked by the kids in my CRE (Christian Religious Education) class many times how old I was when I understood there was a God. I couldn't really answer that, but the thing I did know was that there was something, or someone, out there keeping an eye on things, and that someone had me in their care. My grandma had taught me that this was Jesus, and she taught me a prayer that I used to say every night:

> Gentle Jesus,
> meek and mild,
> look upon a little child;
> pity my simplicity,
> suffer me to come to Thee.

I would then ask God for the things that I wanted. I must say that I never really got the pony, or the bride doll, that I asked for. But, at times when things were really bad and scary, I would say the prayer and, somehow, things turned out okay.

Then my grandfather died. I was four at the time, and had been sent down to my nana in Ocean Grove as, once again, Dad and Mum had split up. My dad borrowed a car and drove down to Ocean Grove to pick me up so I could say goodbye to Papa, who was dying.

When I was taken into the room my nan explained that the noise that pa was making was called 'the death rattle', and not to be frightened as it would go on for a while and meant nothing. I saw the man on the bed. I didn't see my pa. I remembered I was frightened, and so scared when I looked at him. Nana took my hand, and moved me forward, telling me to kiss him goodbye. I didn't want to, I didn't want to kiss this man, but I did.

I said "Goodbye, man, you are not my pa!" I wonder if Pa understood, or if he really thought I didn't like him, and so I had missed my opportunity to say goodbye, and to tell him just how much I loved him. Little did I know then that this 'death-rattle' thing would be a part of my life; something that would be with me many times, and something that I always seemed to mess up.

When my dad drove me home after we visited pa dying, he told me to look back and look for a red light. I saw it and yelled "There it is!"

From the top of the Leopold Hill I could see a red light and Dad told me that it was Papa lighting a cigarette. I felt really happy, and figured that God had heard me, and that my Pa would be alive tomorrow – the real Pa not the man on the bed making the horrible noises.

He died that night.

I stopped saying my prayer for Pa after that and somehow, as time when on, I forgot things. From time to time I tell stories about my Pa, like how he told me that, in the Anzac story of Simpson and his donkey, he called Simpson 'Simmo'. He insisted that the donkey was not called Murphy at all, but was called 'Hee Haw'. Pa went on to explain how he would get up in the morning in Gallipoli and wave to Simmo, and Simmo would offer him a ride on Hee Haw.

He loved galloping along the beach on Hee Haw waving to his friends as he went. Naturally, I went to school and told them all about Pa and Simmo, and how they had got the story wrong. I had, however, some credibility in that I wore my Pa's medals, and so what happened next seemed possible to them. Apparently, as my nana told us all later, the school rang Pa and asked him if he would speak next ANZAC day.

Pa told wonderful stories; he never read them, just made them up. He taught me how to fight, explaining to me that when their mouths were open, you needed to hit them on the chin in an upward motion, and that was called an upper-cut. I would put all my dolls to sleep, and then Pa would wake them up, and be allowed to hit Pa. Weird.

I hated his funeral. I was angry, but said nothing to anyone, and couldn't even cry, even though my nana kept saying, "Just let it go pet… It will be better outside than in." Whatever that meant. Others kept saying what a brave person I was for one so young! This was the first time that I felt that God had let me down, and the first time my prayer hadn't worked. I tried to put it to one side, and tried to remember the times when God had come through, and was real, very real.

There was one particular episode that stood out. I could remember clearly that God was so real, and helped me. I can't remember why, but all three of us were living together at my aunt's in Newtown. She had a very big house, and I had just started school at Ashby, prior to living at Aunty Lily. Nana's place was near Ashby (the three of us and were living with my aunt).

One particular time I remember well. We were living with my aunt in Newtown, and I had to get to school almost five kilometres down Pakington

Street. I was in prep grade and, although I had begun prep from Nan and Papa's place, we had moved to my aunt's as my mother had caused trouble at nana's and didn't get on with my uncle's new wife. How awful this must have been for my nana, whose husband had just died, and had Dad, Mum and me, along with her other son and his wife, living in the one house.

My cousin was supposed to take me on the cross-bar of his bicycle, which we called 'dinking', each morning, and then dink me home. However, on this occasion, he didn't come. I waited and waited, until it was almost dark. I made the decision to walk, and started out, not knowing exactly where I was going except that I had to go up a huge hill. Every morning he would dink me down the hill, and I was so scared that I would shut my eyes and say my prayer. I knew he hated having to do this, and I knew that he also hated me.

Tonight I said the same prayer, and just started walking, pretending in my head that I was walking along with someone. That someone I called Jesus, from the prayer. I am not sure what really happened but, somehow, I managed to find the right the hill, managed the turn, and walked into my aunt's place, to find everyone yelling at everyone else.

My dad started first, saying that I didn't wait for Barry. I denied this, and so my mum called Barry a liar, and then she and my aunt started yelling at each other. I finally yelled for them to stop, and told them that there was no need to worry because I had prayed to God, as Nana had taught me, and Jesus had shown me the way home. Everyone stood in disbelief.

"She's weird, Jean. Really weird," my father said, as he shook his head.

I quietly marched off to bed. I could still hear them arguing, but this time it was just my mother and father.

"If you were any kind of mother you would have been at the school, and picked her up, instead of boozing with your drunken seamen mates," I heard my dad say.

Right on cue the record player went on, and 'Irene Goodnight' came wafting through the rooms. My dad walked out, slamming the front door. My mum called a taxi, and she went out. I climbed into bed, only to see my cousin, Barry, standing at the doorway, running his finger across his throat indicating what would happen to me. All I could do was poke out my tongue.

The next day I was packed off to nana's. Yea!!! We were leaving my aunt's.

There were so many times this scenario happened when, as a family, we would get back together. Then, bingo, the split would happen, and I could be sent to nana's usually, with Dad as it was his mother. I would stay there each time until they reunited again, and then off we would go to relatives, or sometimes just all stay at Nana's, or sometimes get a flat or house. It didn't really matter, though, wherever we were I knew that it would only be for a short time, and then the process would begin again.

Chapter 5

The final split

I don't know what caused it, as I wasn't there. Mum and Dad both had black eyes. Mum moved out from Nana's, but Dad and I stayed and life was wonderful. When Dad came home on Saturday nights, if the horses had run well, then wonderful things would happen. I would be taken to the shop on the corner, and given a free hand to buy lollies and comics. Everyone was a winner. If the horses went badly then Dad wouldn't come home till late, but I wouldn't hear him.

I was doing pretty well at school, so I am told, and life was fine. I didn't see much of Mum and then, suddenly, she started to call around. She and Dad always seemed to be talking about things, and I naturally assumed that we would all be getting back together. I didn't take much notice until one day I was summoned to the dining room.

My nana was crying, and hugged me so hard, sobbing, "I'm sorry, Pet." My parents looked at me, then started to explain what would happen. It appeared that Mum had found another man. He was known as 'Sticky', and was a seaman. She had decided to get a divorce and marry him. My dad explained that he would be going to Perth to start a new life. I looked at them both, realizing that, somehow, I didn't fit into this equation. For a moment I dared to hope… Would I be staying with Nana for good?

Not so. Dad went on to explain that, if I had have been a boy, he would have taken me but, because I was a girl, I was going to Adelaide with my mother to start a new life with this man called Sticky. I had been banking the money that Nan, and other people, had been giving me for birthdays, tooth fairies, etc and my mother told me to go and get my bank book, as she would be borrowing this to help pay for our airfares. I can't remember exactly how much I had, but I do remember, in later life, she gave me her sewing machine saying that this would repay the money she borrowed, way back then. It's funny the little things in life we all remember, isn't it?

At the airport there were lots of tears, lots of promises, and we boarded the plane to head to South Adelaide where this new life would begin. She said everything would turn out okay, because this Sticky was a wonderful person, whom Mum loved, and who loved her. I can remember thinking to myself that, if everything was going to be so wonderful, then why was Nana crying so hard, and where was my dad in all of this?

It wasn't until my teenage years that I realized why Nan was crying. She had met this Sticky the week, before as Mum insisted she should. When she asked him what he did for living, he produced a gun from inside his pocket. Nan told me this story when I asked about him in later years because, even though he featured in my life when Mum was around, he never material-ized in my life at all. I never saw him.

On one occasion, I remember Mum was standing in The Avenue, in Ocean Grove, looking out to the ocean with a candle in her hand. I was given the candle, and she produced a sheet which she fluttered across the candle, and claimed that she was signalling to his ship as it passed through the Heads. She was also convinced that he had messaged her. He'd also appeared in her life a lot when she was really schitzo (suffering from schizophrenia). Apparently he had satisfied her sexually, in lots of ways that I really don't want to remember, but often she would be on the bed, gravitating and screaming at me to get out as she was having sex with Sticky. When she was in the various mental homes, she would write letters addressed to different ships that she thought he was on, but he never answered.

Chapter 6

—

A New Life Begins
(6 years – 8 years)

I can't remember too much about the flight over to Adelaide, or getting to where we were staying. For that matter, ever meeting the magnificent Sticky. I don't think I ever did. However, I do remember Mum taking me to the bank, and signing a form to get out what money I had in my school account.

We set up house in the country, near Adelaide, where Mum was employed as a sort of housekeeper. This is when the fun and games really began to happen. I guess, if I look back, it was this particular time in my life that set the pattern for many of the insecurities that I feel today. It was a short period of time, but a dramatic one for a seven-year-old girl, and I guess too, because I was that little bit older. I remember much of what happened, vividly. Even today I often have dreams or flashbacks. For the first time ever, I was on my own, with no grandparents to run to, and nobody really that I could trust. I loved my mum but, at this tender age, I began to understand that the way she often behaved was not normal. I knew that I had to keep one step ahead of her to ensure that I was safe.

We arrived at this old house in the country and, it appeared to me, that my mum was to be a domestic for an elderly man and woman. Together we had a room which we shared, and the yard was huge so there was plenty of space to run and play. For a while there was no trouble, and things were going okay. The elderly man had given me a couple of rabbits that he had caught, and I got to feed them, pretend they were my children, and teach them school. I would often sit outside the hutch and read to them.

Obviously, everyone forgot that I was supposed to go to school, that this year I was to be in Year 2 because I had started Prep at aged four. I kept telling Mum in the hope that she would send me off, but something always came up.

"Don't worry about it, Chicko," she would say. "Just let us all settle in, and then we'll see about school later."

Chicko was a name that she called me, and relatives also called me 'Chick'. The reason for this goes back to when my Pa died and, to console me, Nan bought me a couple of day-old chickens at the Cressy market in Geelong to take my mind off things. Unfortunately they all died and, as each one passed away, it was replaced with another. Apparently I would insist that each one have a special burial in a chocolate box, and be placed in a grave in the garden accompanied by a prayer and a song. The story goes that some 20 chicks were buried there, most of them never seeing the light of day.

As first, life on the farm was okay. The old man was nice, but I was careful to never let him get too close to me. His wife was nasty, and I can't recall her calling me anything other than "that little brat!"

We often visited Audrey, a friend of Mum's. She was okay to me, but I remember her feeding me potted meat and chocolate milk, and me vomiting my heart out for two days. I have never eaten it since! She lived in a sort of bungalow, behind a large house in a little lane in South Adelaide. I didn't know then, but I suspect it was a sort of brothel, as often there would be many people there, mainly men. I used to like playing with some young children from the big house at the front. Their father was always home, and he seemed to be in control of everyone, including Mum and Audrey. His kids were younger so, of course, this naturally made me the boss, which I loved.

One night, when we came home from visiting Audrey's, I found all my rabbits gone. They had been let out of the hatch. I was upset, and so I ran inside crying. My mum wasn't there at the time, and the old lady just laughed and said she had done it. She said to tell my mum that, if she didn't behave herself, other things would happen.

I told mum, and she laughed. The next two days Mum wouldn't let me eat any food from the table, as she said that the lady was trying to poison us with Ratsack. We brought biscuits, etc, and ate them in our room. One sunny afternoon, Aunty Audrey came over, and Mum, Audrey, and the old man, went to the beach, which wasn't that far away. I was just mucking around, when I heard the crack of a gun and, as I looked up, I saw the old lady running toward Mum and Audrey, screaming. The old man had run off, and Mum grabbed my hand and, with Audrey, we raced along the beach. We didn't even go to the house to get our stuff, we just ran. From then on, home was to be Aunty Audrey's. Apparently, that gun was full of saltpetre, not bullets. Mum and Audrey went back later that week, and collected our stuff. It was tied up in a damask table cloth that Mum had as a wedding present. I still have the table cloth today!

As the bungalow was small, Audrey and Mum slept in the double bed at night, and I had a bed on the floor. Sometimes a man might get in the big bed, and Mum would tell me to just be very quiet and to pull the blankets over my head. This didn't happen that much, so life was okay. Now we were living with Audrey, a great thing happened. I got to go to school.

The kids from the house in front went off every day to school, and I think the man from that house had something to say about me being around all the time.

I especially remember one weekend when Mum was minding all the children in the big house in the front of the bungalow, and obviously having a bad attack of the 'voices'. She decided that I was spoilt, and that I needed to know what it was to have nothing, like the kids that I was playing with. The decision was made that these little kids needed to be bathed, and have clean clothes – my clothes. Each child was bathed, and played with in the bath. I was not allowed in until the end. The water was brown and cold, and I hated it. I still grimace today when I think about it, as I was a clean little thing. Finally I got in but, after finishing, there were no clothes left. I was made to run from the old house to the bungalow in the nude to get clothes, while all the others just stood there looking. I can still feel the shame of this.

Maybe that's why I really hate my body, and am not comfortable with people touching it. My best friend, Kozzie, often laughs when she gives me a cuddle and I tell her be careful, my body is a temple not to be hugged vigorously or looked at.

I think the lesson that I was supposed to learn was that I was spoilt, and had everything, while these kids had nothing. But that didn't make sense, even then. As time went on I learnt, where possible, to just go along with Mum when she was in her bi-polar state. But to an eight-year-old, that was asking too much, and sometimes I got frightened and angry.

Despite the bathing incident, I was excited because, at last, I was to go to school on the Monday. I remember that, when I had been at school previously, teachers had told me I was quite clever, and I got to be a monitor and do special things. I knew I could read well, because Mrs Russell at Ashby had picked me out, of all the kids in Year 2, to read out a special poem on ANZAC day, usually given to an older child.

Off I went to school, but I was a bit confused with the first class as it was drawing. We had very special drawing books, with tissue paper between each page. Something I had never seen before. That day we were to draw a ball and colour it in. "Easy peasy," I think to myself. I had my ball done and dusted within about five minutes, and sat up with my pastels packed, ready to receive what, I perceived, would be my reward. The teacher marched up, grabbed my book, and held it up to everyone, announcing loudly to the whole class that this was the worst she had ever seen, as it had no 'shading'. In fact, it was nothing at all except a yellow circle! What did she want?! It was a yellow ball, and it didn't need lights. The class laughed, and she threw my book back, narrowly missing my head.

I didn't cry! I remembered staring ahead, and thinking to myself that this Adelaide school was stupid, and I wouldn't be coming here again.

What we learn really stays with us in some ways. I still can't draw to save myself. I was obsessed with horses, and I can draw a mean horse, but all my horses only have two legs. My father used to ask, "Where's its other legs?" I gave up trying to explain to people that each leg was in front of the other, so you didn't need to draw four!

I didn't go back to school, as luck or destiny would have it. There was a party at the big house for Easter that night, and we were all going. There was lots of drinking, and many drunk people.

I got tired and sick of playing with the kids, and Mum was kind of away with the fairies, so I just hopped in a cot that was spare, and went to sleep. I knew we would be sleeping over so, thoughtfully, I had packed my case with clean knickers for the morning, just in case. My beautiful paisley school case, that Nana had given me, lay beside me in the cot.

The man woke me up the next morning. There was mess everywhere, and it smelled of stale tobacco. He told me he was sorry, but I would have to go, as I couldn't stay there because he had too many children to feed. I asked where my mum was, and he took my hand and led me outside. He pointed to a bush that was squashed. By now he had been joined by his wife, and some kids.

"She slept there last night, with the Easter Bunny," he said. "And we don't know where she is."

I said that I would go to Aunty Audrey's, but he told me that Audrey didn't live there anymore. No one spoke much, so I just picked up my case (I had already put on my clean knickers), and headed for the door.

"Where are you going?" he asked and, without a moment's hesitation, I replied, "I am going home to my Nana's in Geelong, Victoria, and marched out. I heard him laughing, and I was determined that this would be the end of my stay in Adelaide. I was heading home.

I walked and walked for what seemed to be forever and, finally, sat in a bus station. I noticed that a car had been driving alongside me for a while, but far enough back that I couldn't see.

I nestled into the bus stop to have a rest when the car pulled up, and two policewomen got out. They walked over and started to ask me questions, like who was I, and where was I going.

I told them everything, because Nana had told me that police were there to help people. I hoped they somehow might get Nana to bring me home. The tall one finally told me that they had found my mother, that she was on a ship in nothing but a towel. She had been taking pot plants from outside the door of the cabins, and putting them back inside. I didn't understand what this really meant, but I knew that, once again, Mum was off on a tangent.

They put me in the car and took me to the police station, where they said my mum was. I was given something to eat, and they treated me well. Finally another policewoman came in, and told me to take off my clothes, as Mum had told them I had ringworm. I told her that I didn't have ringworm, and she slapped me and called me a liar, and started to rip off my cardigan. I was hanging on to everything as tight as I could but, in the end, I gave up and let her strip me naked. I stood on the table stark naked, while she checked every crevice of my body. Again I felt very embarrassed, because others were watching and I felt so vulnerable. No ringworms were found!

"Bloody Adelaide! Stupid bloody schools! And now stupid fucking police!" The one thing I had learnt from Adelaide was to use swear words.

Mum was charged, and I understood that I was to be taken to a home where I would stay indefinitely until her case was heard, and then a decision would be made as to which institution I would be sent to.

Chapter 7

The Home (still 8)

It was okay, I guess. Of all the things about it though, I will never eat black stew again! I am not sure what the place was, but it seemed like a type of holding pen. There were a couple of handicapped children there, and quite a few girls that were about 15. One of them told me that they were there to learn some manners and things, because soon they would be allowed out to work and live on their own. Somehow they just took hold of me, and I can probably have them to thank for the good thing that happened from there.

I remember one night, a girl was brought in and put in a cell (these were out the back). She was screaming and yelling, and wanted the toilet. I ran to get one of the girls, who told her that she had to go in the pot provided, and told me I was never to go out there again.

I also had a very important job. I was their spy. At night they had magazines called 'True Confession' and, after lights out, they would use torches to read them. I was having night tremors, so my bed was put nearest the door. That was so the person on duty could hear me if I screamed. I became their spy and, when the nurse moved to check, I would warn them.

I kept writing letters to my nanas, and to my dad, on every piece of paper I could get my hands on. One of the girls promised me that she would post the letters herself when she got out, and I never really found out if it was her, or just the authorities and their procedures, that brought my nan to Adelaide.

It was announced that the court case would be coming up, and the girls were so excited. They constantly tutored me in saying "Yes judge, no judge", etc, and making me smile, as they said I always looked angry. The clothes that I came in, particularly a jumper that my mother had knitted me, were washed meticulously, and I was made to wear orphanage clothes until these could be produced. I will always remember that my white sandals were cleaned with tooth paste, and I was told that it was important that I look clean and respectable, as though I belonged somewhere.

I looked across, for the last time I hoped, at the big orphanage over the road. One of the nurses, who had caught me staring across, kept telling me that it wouldn't be long before I was there, as that was where kids went when they didn't have families.

Finally D Day came, and the police car arrived to take me to the court. To my surprise, sitting in the back was my mum. No kisses, hugs, or how you going, or anything, just a blank stare, and a comment that I had better say the right things, and not say some things or we would all end up in jail.

I never knew why exactly we would go to jail, but I figured it was because of what Aunty Audrey and Mum did with the men that came in, and I also imagined that the man with the house and kids, probably did bad things.

We walked into the courtroom and there, across from where we were, was my Nana Tompkins (Mum's mother) who had come to Adelaide to, hopefully, save me. The story goes that both nanas wanted to come, but it was felt that Nana Read was probably not in as good a financial situation as my Nana Tompkins. Everyone was unsure how long this would take, so finances played a large part.

I never wondered, until now as I am writing this, why my dad didn't come? Wouldn't a father, who loved his daughter, come and get her? I didn't care because there, in front of me, was hope; a chance to get out of this stupid place they called Adelaide. Nana didn't come towards me at all, but she smiled and I knew it was going to be okay. On the other hand, my mum was scowling at Nana, and I knew they never got along much anyway.

I was in the court throughout the trial, but I didn't understand much until, suddenly, everyone was looking at me. The judge was asking me to come towards him, as he wanted to ask me questions. My heart pounded, and I heard the voices and the panic, "Tell them nothing! Use your manners. Smile more! We might all end up in jail." And, once more in my head, I reached for my prayer "Gentle Jesus, meek and mild…" It was going to be all right, or was it?

I really didn't listen much to what was said in the court or, if I did, I can't remember. I do remember, though, a policewoman leading me towards the judge.

The first thing he said to me was, "That's a beautiful jumper. Who knitted it for you?"

I remember feeling relieved the girls had been right all along. I had to look clean and well kept. I hope he noticed my shoes, which were cleaned spotlessly with the toothpaste.

"My mum," I answered his question politely, and added that she was a wonderful knitter.

Mum smiled and looked happy, and the judge said, "Well she can't be all that bad of a mother, can she Nola?"

I didn't say anything at all, but I saw Mum stare straight at my grandma. I don't remember any of the other questions, but I don't think I said anything bad, or anything that Mum would be unhappy with. Finally, the judge looked at me and said what a bright sensible girl I was, and he thought that I could make a decision that would help him make up his mind as to what would happen to me.

He gave me the choice of going home with Nana or staying in Adelaide. I saw Mum move forward, and I felt kind of weird. I wanted my mum, and I loved her, but the thought of staying meant that I would be going to the permanent place across the oval, for how long no one knew. And then what? Back to Aunty Audrey's? Would this magical Sticky come and claim us? Would we move somewhere else? Who would know? I was just so frightened, and then I looked at Nan. Home to Ocean Grove meant safety, love, school friends, and I could visit my other nana whenever I wanted. Maybe my dad would be there.

I looked up and replied, "I want to go with Nan."

It was decided then and there, and Nana was allowed to come and get me. I walked toward Mum to give her a kiss, but that was not going to happen. She looked so angry. "You sold me out, Chick!" These were her words, but I didn't understand what she meant until much later in life.

I think these were the words that indicated that she never forgave me for choosing nana above her. That's not what I meant but, to Mum I think, she kept that in her heart always, and I'm not sure that she ever forgave me and we never really talked about it. In fact, now that I write this, we never ever talked about my early life at all, even though I looked after her for many years before she died. She would never really admit to anything, saying always I couldn't have done that! Or I must have had the voices, all of which gave her an excuse, but left me never really knowing whether she loved me and forgave me for not picking her. As she walked away with the policewoman we had come with, I knew that I had done the wrong thing, but I was fighting, fighting for my survival, and a normality of some kind.

We had to stay in Adelaide for a couple of days, and that was fun as Nana took me to see a Ma and Pa Kettle movie. I had forgotten what it was to laugh, and I laughed and laughed. We ate out in cafés, which was also fun, and at a big cafeteria thing where you walked around and picked out your food. We went to see Mum, and she was in a much better mood. She gave me a cuddle and a kiss, and showed me the children in another room that she would have to look after. She said she was sick and would stay there until she got better, and then she would come and get me from Nana's.

I never really understood about the custody thing, but I overheard Nana saying that Mum was found to be an unfit and proper mother, so Nana was granted legal custody. I heard my other Nana (Dad's mother) and her fighting one day about this, and Nana Read said that this could not happen as my dad was my legal custodian, and he had relinquished nothing. She told Nana that he was coming home, and the rest of the stuff I didn't hear much of. During the many times that Mum lived at home with us, her and Nan would fight about this and other things, and Mum would insist that she had never lost custody. Mum also believed that Nan loved Mum's brother much more than her, and that Nana gave Mum nothing as a child. Many times I would listen in, and believed Mum then but, when I look through records now, I see that she danced at the Ballarat Eisteddfods, played netball and, I think, really had a pretty good life. Mum wanted to leave school, but she said that Nana made her leave. I knew that wasn't true, and probably just a figment of her 'voices'.

Chapter 8

9 – 12 years

Life in Ocean Grove with Nana and Pop was good. I went to school, and this time it was a school that didn't have drawing, so I was able to take up my position again as one the brightest pupils.

I think I changed a lot because, for some reason, I was always in trouble. I answered teachers back, and ran away from school with my friend, Beila.

Nan spent time at the school, explaining that I had had a pretty bad life, and so I think I actually got away with more than I should. I was also left with bad dreams; dreams I still have sometimes. Maybe someone might tell me what that means.

Lots of good things happened during my time at nanas. I was about nine when I got there, and 14 when I left to go to live with my dad.

My friend, Beila, lived over the road from us, and I think his parents were Yugoslavia. He didn't speak much English though, but he and I understood each other and he was my protector. Nana and Beila never got on, and he would never come inside. One day they had words, because Nana had growled at me for something, and clipped me under the ear.

Beila moved forward with a cross look on his face and announced, "I will kaput you!"

When I asked him what this meant, he replied, "Cut her bloody head off!"

No one at school could touch me, or look out, Beila was there. I loved any kind of sport, and I would often play football with the boys. Beila wouldn't play, but would just walk around the oval, watching. If anyone came near me, and tackled me, then look out!

Naturally I was the star! Probably sport was the thing that made me. The kids knew that I had been in an 'orphanage', and that I lived with my elderly grandparents. Often I could be neglected by the 'pretty people'. I didn't get to go their parties much but, if ever they needed a team member for tennis, basketball, or anything competitive, you could bet I was one of the first picked.

I did get to go to one party though. She was the coolest girl in the school and in Year 6, while I was in Year 5, but she always picked me in her netball team. I was so excited that Nan made a new dress, and off I went with strict instructions on how to behave. Apparently I had a habit of sniffing, and so Nana had pinned a handkerchief on to my dress just in case. This, of course, went with the camphor bag around my neck!!! When we sat at the table I noticed, on the bread-and-butter plate, that there was a white handkerchief. Obviously I was horrified. I had been sniffing, and the girl's mother had seen fit to provide me with a handkerchief. I blew my nose on it, and then stuck it up my sleeve. No problems! Ha! When I got home the white thing fell out while I was getting undressed, and Nana picked it up and laughed. She explained that it was what was called a napkin. We didn't have napkins at home, but had to wash our face and hands before and after we had finished eating. I didn't think much about it until I got to school the next morning.

There they were standing at the gate. A boy that I fancied called out "Here comes snotty wottie!" Beila wasn't around, but I knew immediately that the girls had told everyone about the napkin, and they were standing there giggling. I walked straight up to him, and punched him fair and square in the nose. Naturally Nan was called to the school, and I was made to apologize, as I had broken his nose. His mother, for the rest of my school life, never looked at me or spoke to me again.

We had a teacher whom we all thought wore makeup on his face. I think now the poor man had pimples but, never-the-less, he was quite nasty, and stickler for picking up papers during lunch. Usually I went home for lunch but, being the hero that I am and wanting to prove myself to the 'girls', I decided to stay on his duty day and give him a bit of curry.

As he walked along, I was behind him mimicking his very effective walk. People were laughing, and I was enjoying it also. Each time he turned I would diligently pick up papers and smile at him. Unfortunately, one time I was a bit slow. He caught me, grabbed me by the shoulder, and marched me to the door, telling me to go to the office. As I walked through the door he stood there, but the door did not shut.

"Close the door!" he yelled, and turned away.

"Close the F… door yourself," I replied, obviously not quietly enough.

He went crazy, dragging me down the corridor screaming. I was only a little thing, not the big bopper that I am today. The headmaster got me and, of course, he gave me the strap. But I think the teacher also got into trouble, as I heard them yelling in the office at each other. That teacher never came back, and our new teacher was wonderful. She was old, and her entire teaching skill was base around chocolate! If you were good, you got chocolate. If you were bad and stopped doing what you were doing, you would get a chocolate. Every day we made puppet dolls. Life was wonderful. Sometimes in the afternoon I was called out to the prep teacher's room, and I would take the preps for stories, songs and, can you believe it, ART. Crazy art…

"Draw what you like for art, kids!" "Oh, that is so beautiful. You are so talented!" No stupid static shaded balls for my class. Just be free and draw anything! We were not in stupid South Australia now.

The prep teacher was the wife of the principal, and she lived over the road. She would often go home to take her washing off the clothes line, and do odd jobs. She was also my music teacher and, I think, I was her star pupil.

Chapter 9

Home Life (9 – 12)

Ocean Grove was home, with Nan and Pop (Mum's parents). At least that was something that remained consistent. I stayed there for some eight years, and it meant that school consistency was also now existent. My home life, although stable, was a weird one in some respects. At one stage in their two-bedroom house, we had my great grandmother and my mother, as well as me living there. My Nan, on my mother's side, unlike my other Nana, seemed a cold type of person in some ways, but now when I look back, I see her magnificence and her generosity. I understand now why she kept her feelings to herself, as I now understand how, in her own way, she loved me.

She had three well-off sisters, and also a brother. All had large home, all were married, and all fairly wealthy. With all these assets, it was only Nan who took her mother in when she became demented. In itself, this was difficult as, in some ways, great grandma could be a little dangerous. She detested me, and used to snarl at me, because I would often dob her in for doing things that I knew would get her into trouble. Once she put the iron away in the cupboard without unplugging it, which nearly burnt the kitchen down. She was also notorious for going down to the shops, mainly the butchers, and buying heaps of meat and things, and then giving them for just one penny. Nana would then have to pay up. When we got TV in 1956, great grandmother was beside herself. One day we came home to find her behind the TV with a collection of Christmas cards, trying to give them to the man on the screen.

When I asked what she was doing, she said, "That lovely man keeps giving me a cup of tea, but Ada (my Nana) won't let me take it, so I'm giving him a present."

They were weird things, but the worst thing of all was that she would mess herself, and then deny it. The smell would waft around, and then she would try and clean herself up with rags, and throw the rags in a box under her bed which was next to mine. Nan would have to bath her, and put clean clothes on her, but she never complained.

There were also times when my mum came home to live with us, and often arguments would start up between Nan and her about custody. They also argued about things that Mum had done. Nana kept reminding her that she had spent heaps of money picking up the pieces of Mum's escapades, and then it would be on for young and old.

Most of the time I liked it when Mum was home. It usually meant that the dresses that she sewed for me were quite modern. I would also win the decorated saucer competition at the CWA fête, and the main prize at the fancy dress ball. I always wanted to go as a pretty princess but Mum said the important thing was to show the judges that time and effort went in to the presentation. One year I won as a sewing basket. It took Mum weeks to sew on all the things, like pins, etc, and the judges were most impressed.

Mum's visits weren't always that long. Once I saw her start to go out in Geelong, and make herself a couple of black and white dresses, then I knew it wouldn't be long before she didn't came home. In high school, Mum wasn't around much at all, and Nana and Pop said she had to stay in hospital for a long time – some three years. She was at the asylum in Ballarat, and we went to see her. I hardly recognized her. She was drugged, and simply lay on the floor. I didn't go again.

As high school started, I lost some of my friends from Ocean Grove as I seemed to slip naturally in the city kids' world of sports. Beila Bob, my best friend from primary school, left just before we were to go to high school. Beila Bob and his family left without even saying goodbye! He may have gone, but I will never forget him.

The classic Beila story, which must be told, is of our Year 6 concert. Our teachers had written a play based on the Desert Song. I had a main part but, because the school was small, everyone became either a member of the foreign legion, or a member of the Red Shadows' gang. Beila and I, of course, were in the Red Shadows' gang. It really didn't matter how many times I told him that this was just a play, and we were only acting. He just didn't get it.

"We must win 'Ready'. We must win at all costs!"

"No, Beila." I would try to explain how the Foreign Legion wins. He would always look sad and shake his head, and hardly raise his sword. But this all changed on the actual night. As the song started, "Ho, that's the sound that comes to warn you so!" we raced onto the stage. I think Beila was completely overtaken by emotion! He crashed through everyone to the leader of the Foreign Legion, and then proceeded to belt him with his sword. Blood was spilt, teachers panicked, the curtains came down, and the play was halted until order was restored. Unfortunately, without Beila.

But just like that he was gone. Beila Bob had been my protector and, even though he spoke very little English, I understood him. Our rabbit sales stopped, no more adventures on the weekends, and I was now in Year 7.

My childhood was over. Life would be OK now .... or would it?

Chapter 10

___

Is this enough for Sarah?

I wondered if this was enough. How much of my life did Sarah, the psychiatrist, want? This is my childhood, but was it enough to work out what the catalyst was that started my panic and depression. The strange thing was that, when I read it through a number of times, it brought back memories that I had forgotten and had put aside. It brought back things I had not spoken much to anyone about.

I rang Sarah, and made an appointment for the next day. I told her I had finished the early years, and wondered if that was enough. She indicated that would work with that and see where it led us. She asked if I could drop what I had written into her office that afternoon so she could read it through.

When I walked in the following day for my appointment, I looked at her face and knew immediately that there was something strange.

She walked over, grabbed me, and gave me the biggest hug I have ever had.

"How did you survive? However did you manage to turn out the way you did? Don't you know you're a miracle!"

I was taken back, and remained speechless for a while.

"It was nothing special," I said. "It was probably just the same as what everyone else had in their lives."

She shook her head. "I don't think so," she said with a chuckle. "No, you really should do something about this, but now is not the time. Let's look for some of the things that you coped with, and some of the decisions you made as a child that kept you safe. Decisions that involved moral and social judgements. Decisions that you should never have had to make as a child, but you did.

"Tell me", she said. "As an eight-year-old child, how did you think you were going to get to Victoria, and find your Nana?"

I thought for a moment and then said: "I really don't know but I knew, just as I got home when my cousin had forgotten to pick me up, that somehow God would find a way to take care of me, just as Nana had told me. So I just kept saying my prayer… *Gentle Jesus, meek and mild, look upon a little child; pity my simplicity, suffer me to come to Thee.*"

She gave me a wiry smile and replied: "Nola, your faith was incredible. Somehow there is something special about you, and something incredible in your story that leads you forward."

I knew I was recognised as a good teacher, and then as a principal. At one stage, I was the president of the Primary Principals Association in my home town. I also understood that I had played a number of sports at a reasonably high level (due to my competitive nature), but had never considered these as any major achievements.

We talked for a while about the mini strategies, as a child, I'd unknowingly used to cope with these situations. Sarah felt that, for me, the best strategies that I could use I already knew, and could use them successfully. What she felt was important, and a strategy that I had not applied before, was that I needed to learn to cut myself some slack, and to start thinking how wonderful I actually was? I laughed, and I found it very amusing. Never thought of myself in this light before, and I found it embarrassing.

"I can't do that," I said. "It would be like skiting."

Sarah's answer came as somewhat of a surprise. "I know what you can do," she said. "Why don't you just go on with your story, and see what happens. Read through this and see if you can learn to love the little girl in the story. Recognise just how wonderful she is, and then write what becomes of her. What have you got to lose, and who cares if it takes forever. Just keep writing."

We said goodbye, and she told me that if ever needed her to just make an appointment. She wanted to see me again in six months to see how things were going.

I left her office and came home. I sat down and I started thinking about my day.

· I've found the only picture I had as baby, and looked at it long and hard. Mum's right, my hair looked as though it had been cut by lawn mower, and I certainly looked a bit boofy. Maybe I wasn't hers, as she had suggested many times. Maybe I belonged to someone else? The more I looked at the picture, the more I started to smile. Not pretty, but cute.

When I got in the shower that night, I started to think about that little girl, and just how brave she had been. Suddenly the tears started to fall down. I love you, little girl, I whispered. You are really beautiful.

For the first time I noticed, when I went to bed, how I was curled up. I was curled into a ball, with my arms entwined around my breasts. This is how I slept every night, and now I knew why ... I was protecting and cuddling myself. As a little girl, I had needed someone had to hold and love me.

Chapter 11

——

High School Begins (12 – 15 years)

I loved school, and tried out for everything. Fortunately I was good at sport, so made the netball, softball teams, etc. Coming from the bush, this was quite an achievement in Year 7, as most of the kids were already involved in Saturday sport.

The other interesting thing about this time of the year was that Dad had appeared on the scene. He started to come down to Ocean Grove on Sundays and, during these visits, we would play tennis, throw softballs, and play any type of competitive sport. I thought I was good, but never once did I beat him at anything. His visits would be capped off by a huge pineapple milkshake while waiting for the bus. I never wanted him to go, and was really disappointed when he didn't come down on the Sunday.

At school, somehow I seemed to mix with a whole different group of people. Most of my friends were in Geelong, and sport had given me a whole new peer group. When I think of it, I realised how embarrassed I had felt on the bus trips to and from the Ocean Grove school, as I was often sitting alone.

My school work was okay, except for cookery and sewing. I was banned from cooking when I accidently nearly burnt the cookery centre down. I say accidentally, because it really was a twist of fate. During class, I didn't have enough stewed apples to go into the pie. They tasted so nice I kept eating them raw. As a punishment, the teacher made me stay in at recess, and peel and cook more apples. Unfortunately there was netball practice during recess, but I figured I could do this, and turn my apples down low on the stove. No one would know.

What I didn't account for was that this recess would be extra long, as one of our teachers got sick and an ambulance had to be called. Nor knowing this, I merrily participated in practice, only stopping along with everyone else, when we heard the sirens from the fire engines as they roared up the street, and saw smoke billowing out of the cookery centre. Naturally my dad was called, and it was announced that I would no longer be doing cookery. Instead I would report to the library.

I often tell people that this experience was the reason that I am considered to be an awful cook. Along with cooking, my other failure was needlework. I never could get the hang of it but, when the teacher found out that my Nana had actually darned the sock that I was given 10/10 for, that was it. Back to the library!

Even in adulthood, I tried to create some sort of domestic skill. Given my background, and the fact that both Mum and my grandmother were excellent sewers, I decided perhaps sewing was actually my calling. After paying my money to have six lessons on stretch sewing with an actual teacher, and finally making a windcheater that fell apart, I was devastated when she told me not to come back, as there were some people who could sew and others that just had no idea. She suggested that I would be wasting my time and money, as well as hers, as I had broken two machines by sewing over pins. I could never see the point of tacking. To me, it was a duplication that wasn't necessary, and that took extra time.

Generally life rolled along, with school going okay, and Dad coming down most Sundays. However, as usual this didn't remain for much longer, and change was coming.

Again my life changed so quickly. My dad came down and said that he had a question to ask me, and that I wasn't to say anything to Nana. He asked if I would come with him to Geelong, and live there if he built us a house. He said Nana Read could come and help look after things. I didn't hesitate, and I could see so many things flash before me. I could play a higher level of sport, and have more opportunities, and I would be living with my dad.

Dad said he had talked about it to Nana. Later that week, Nan took me aside and asked me what I really wanted to do. She pointed out that living with my dad would not be easy, especially because I was a female. I was never to sit on his knee, make sure that the bathroom door was closed, etc. I didn't quite understand because I kept thinking 'This is my dad, not some pervert, so why is she telling me all this?' In later years I found out that Nan had been sexually assaulted by her own father.

It all happened quickly, and I was about to celebrate my 14th birthday. I had my birthday and, for the first time ever, I felt really cool because I could say to people: "This is my dad, and we live here together because my mum has left us." There were quite a few kids in my group whose parents had divorced and separated, but very few who lived with their father. I felt special. Life was okay.

Not long after I moved in, I was to have a birthday. Now, all I needed to make things perfect, was an eggbutt snaffle bridle for my horse. Hints had been given, and I felt sure it was coming. Christmas morning was exciting.

Dad had the string out, and I had to follow it to find my presents. I loved Christmases with Dad.

I followed it to the empty fireplace, and there was a large box. No way could this be the treasured bridle. I shook the box… It rattled, and I smelt it. I ripped off the paper, and there was all this Revlon makeup and stuff.

"Yuck!" Disgusted I threw it on the floor, and continued to follow the string. Another box, but this one was very small. Definitely not a bridle. A marquisate watch was inside.

I looked up at my father, and screamed, "Where's the bridle?"

"It's time you thought about being a lady," he answered. "Your aunt thought these would be exactly what you wanted."

I didn't say anything. I just threw the watch at the fireplace near the smelly stuff, and stomped off to my room. After a short space of time, Dad appeared at the door with the bridle in his hand.

"Come with me," he said. I followed him to the woodshed, where he picked up the axe and proceeded to chop the bridle into little pieces. Not a word was spoken. He marched inside, and I followed him. My lesson on ungratefulness finally learnt. I got nothing for Christmas that year, not even the smelly stuff.

After that Christmas, I started to think about my life as a girl. Periods hadn't yet started, and I was still changing in the toilets with those of us who remained in singlets, as out boobs hadn't yet grown. It was important to wait until this event actually happened rather than cheat with falsies, as one of our number did. She was found in the change room with her petticoat and bra and, inside the bra, were her falsies. Naturally justice had to prevail, so we took the falsies, wrote her name and address, on them and threw them into the boy's toilets.

What horrors we were! I really didn't know anything much about puberty, and what should happen, and how feelings might change. One of the girls in my Year 11 class was pregnant, but was going to finish out the year. I remember she came into the room one day, and went to sit down beside me. I was horrified. Why I don't know, but I shifted. Whenever I went to a public toilet I would actually cover it with paper, in case I caught 'pregnant germs'.

It sounds stupid and naïve but, until my girlfriend and I went to see a film called 'Helga', I thought babies actually came out of your stomach, and that somehow your belly-button popped open. After school I would go down the lane with the guys for a smoke, and we would pinch apples. One day I must have had far too many apples, and I got a stomach ache. When I got home I was moaning.

My dad walked around as though he was lost, and finally said, "Look, when you get to this age you get periods, and often they make your stomach ache. But you will have to go to the chemist and get some pads as you bleed at bit. If you want to know more, just ring your Aunty Rosa."

I looked stunned. I had been told what periods were, and most of my friends had already started menstruating, but I was completely in the dark. Dad thrust a ten-pound note (he was always over generous) and off he went. I looked at the money and thought 'yes, smokes for the week and I won't have to go without lunch'. I thought of having this period thing more often, as it could be quite lucrative.

Nothing happened, and I didn't start menstruating, but I thought it may be best to pretend that I had. Out riding one day my friend, Chris, announced that she would have to stop at the toilet and change her pad. Stupid me suggested that I had better change also. The conversation turned from pads to tampons and Chris (a girl of the world who also had a big sister), produced two tampons and suggested that we try these. We entered the toilets and I starred at the cotton bullet, and wondered how the hell this was going to fit up where it should.

I pushed and pushed and finally managed to get half of it in.

"You ready, Hawkie?" came the question from outside the toilet area. We both mounted the horses and off we went. At first it wasn't too bad but, as we pushed into a trot, you cannot (or maybe you can if you are female) imagine the pain I was in. Tears rolled down my face. I am not sure what exactly happened, but somehow that dreadful thing pushed itself out, and I was free. I decided that day I just wasn't going to have these period things but, underneath, I wondered if something was wrong with me, and that I was born somehow deformed.

Life rolled on easily. Even Mum came home to Nana for a visit, and Dad let her stay with us overnight. On the day of the visit, Mum came with me to the softball. I am not sure what exactly happened, but she was away with the fairies and kept talking to herself. Worst of all, chatting to people she didn't really know. When we got home, she cooked up some kidneys we bought on the way home, and all I can remember was vomiting them up. Finally Dad came home, and found Mum out the back in the toilet. My nana was staying there also, and Mum had Nana up dancing around in the kitchen, and poor Nan was frightened,

Mum refused to come out of the toilet but once Dad appeared, and growled at her. She came out like a little lamb. My other granny and Pop were called, and they came on the motor-bike and side car, and took her home. Finally peace was restored, just Dad, Nana, and me again. After this episode, I think Mum was put into Ballarat again where she stayed for quite a long time.

One day my dad called me in, and sat me down. In his hand he had a letter. He read the letter aloud, it was from Mum. She wanted to come home and live with us, and for her and Dad to try again. I stood there dumbfounded. Dad suggested that perhaps it was worth a try, but he would do whatever it was that I thought should happen. I got up and stomped to my room without saying anything. He stood in the doorway as I began to throw things into a case.

"What are you doing?" he said.

"I am packing," I replied. "And then I am going to get Pop to come and get me because, if she comes, then I go! I am not doing this anymore, Dad!"

"Fair enough," he said. "I'll tell her. Put your things back, and come and help with tea."

In later life, this decision haunted me, and I knew that Mum got the message that I was the one who decided she was not coming home. There are times when I feel that I cheated her out of a happy life, but there were other times when I understand that frightened little girl who had to protect herself.

Although I believed in God, I didn't understand, as I do now, that we do not have to carry this kind of guilt. I John 1:9 says that when we confess our sins God forgives us, and purifies us so we don't have to carry it around. This means that we don't have to let shame and guilt control us, and we can embrace forgiveness, and our identity and worth in Christ

If you think that there is something that you cannot be forgiven, then stop! Please read through John. This passage can be the answer to your feelings of unworthiness.

Chapter 12

Off again!

It was just an ordinary Saturday. I had played tennis in the morning at St Matthews', was going to the gymnasium social after tea with two of my friends, and I had bought a new pair of shoes. They were black and had really pointed toes and a small heel… Very trendy for me.

Dad was home, so was Uncle Sid and another man, which meant that the horses would be happening at my place in the afternoon. For some reason Dad wasn't pencilling for Uncle Sid. For those innocent of gambling, SP bookmaking was illegal, and my dad often wrote up (pencilled the bets) for my uncle, the bookmaker. Our house was a War Service home, which had three large front windows, all of which could be use to watch for police when the races were on.

No one, except Uncle Sid and the penciller, could use the phone or answer it, from 10.00am until 6.00pm on race day. On this particular day, Dad had arranged to go to the football to see Polly Farmer play for Geelong.

As I got ready, I showed them all my shoes, and Dad started to chase me around the house pointing the toes at my bum. The deal was that I would come home after netball, go to my friend's house and then to the gym dance from there. But I had to be home on the 11.00pm bus. Nana had the night off which, I knew she loved, as she could go to her cards.

Off I went to the netball and, as usual after the game, some of us went across to Kardinia Park to see the last quarter of the football match, as we would be able to get in for free. We all stood on the hill watching the game, but suddenly I saw the crowd on the opposite side scatter, and an ambulance appear. A man was being carried around the ground on the inside of the oval.

I felt for the man, and wondered what had happened. When the game finished, I rode home. But as I rode through the gate I felt something was wrong. Nana was there, and so were my aunt and uncle, as well as other people I didn't know. Nana came running, and she was crying. She grabbed me, and all I could work out was that Dad was in hospital. My uncle explained that Dad had had a stroke at the football, and then realised it was my dad they were bringing around the oval. I wished I had known so I could have been with.

Uncle Phil (my dad's brother) took us all to the hospital to see Dad. As I approached the bed, I could see his face and he turned away. I followed him and he tried to speak, but I couldn't understand what he was trying to say.

Finally they gave him a bit of paper, and he wrote on it. He was left-handed and paralysed down the right-hand side. "Don't let them see me like this!" he wrote.

The right-side of his face was twisted and deformed, and I could tell that he was in a real panic. That night we left him, to return the next day. But there was no change, and he had lost consciousness. For the following three days I would go to the hospital after school, but he never gained consciousness again.

I came one day, and a nurse was trying to feed him. But nothing was happening.

"It's a shame about your brother," she said. "Hopefully he won't suffer too much longer."

"Does he have any children, dear?" she asked. Stupid idiot, I thought to myself. Here is a man who had been there for four days, obviously very sick, and yet you don't even know him, and don't even know that he's my dad. I started to get very angry.

Where were the doctors? What were they doing to help him, and why weren't we being told anything? After each visit, Nana said that Dad looked a little better, and that it wouldn't be long before he was back to his old self again as people recover after a stroke. Initially I had believed her, but not now. After what this woman had said, I knew he was going to die.

I went back to school as lunch time was over, and I had basketball practice after school. In the middle of practice, a police car came screeching up Ryrie Street and stopped at the courts. Nana and uncle Phil got out and said we needed to go straight to the hospital, as Dad had taken "a turn for the worse". What could be worse, I wondered. But I wasn't prepared for what I saw when I walked in.

Dad was attached to all sorts of tubes and, on a stand, there was what looked like a balloon thing that was going in and out as he breathed. The balloon would sometimes stop, and I would just stare at it, but Uncle Phil told me to look away, and look at Dad and to tell him things. I started to talk but it was as though he wasn't there. He was white, gaunt, and had sallow eyes. He was not my beautiful handsome father, whose hair was always immaculately combed, and who looked like he had just come out of a band box.

Dad was always immaculate. Even in his work clothes he wore a collar and tie. When asked why, he would say that he did this just case he met the girl of his dreams, his 'Mazza Munroe'. I am told that, when I was born, my dad wanted me named Norma Jean (ring any bells?). My nana, though, registered the birth and signed the certificate, explaining that there was no way I was to be named after that 'tramp', and so changed my name to Nola Jean.

So here I was, starring at my beautiful father who was now gasping for breath.

Then it happened. People ran from everywhere. The loud speaker played the song 'I've been everywhere', and across the top of this came the constant calls for Dr Agar.

"Dr Agar. Immediately. Room two. Code Blue." I got taken outside, and stood there with everyone, including my mother. After what seemed like an endless age, a youngish looking doctor came out and stood in the middle of us all.

"I am sorry to tell you, but Mr Read has passed away."

I was numb. I saw Uncle Phil lurch toward me, but he missed. Then, with all my might, I hauled off and hit the doctor fair in the face, and pushed him to the ground. I think I was kicking, but I am not sure as everything went black. All I can remember after that was waking up in hospital with a young male doctor telling me it would be all right, and that I could go home with him and his wife.

Uncle Phil and Nana appeared, and Uncle Phil was not pleased. Apparently the doctor was not pressing charges, but I would have to apologize. That was not going to happen, I said to myself, and who cares about charges. My intention was to find this missing Agar person and kill her.

I won't bore you with the details because I am not proud of them, but the police did catch me down the lane at the back of the hospital with a large knife. I went to counselling, and somehow things just passed, as did my anger over the time. Why would I be so angry? I couldn't understand why no one cared... The lady feeding Dad didn't know his name, and his doctor couldn't even be bothered coming to help him die. For me this was my only real shot at normality. I had a father who worked, and provided me with a house where everything was normal. Where would I go now? When I have to go into hospital now I am angry, and frightened, and don't behave very well.

Change was about to happen. The funeral was organized, and Dad had no will so, under the law, Mum would get everything he had. She didn't really get that much as there was a War Service Loan on the house, and we had only been in it for 12 months.

My anger was intense. I came home, found as many Bibles as I could, threw them in the fireplace, and lit the fire.

"I hate you God!" I screamed, as my nana tried to hold me and comfort me. "Why have you done this to me? Haven't I put up with enough," I yelled.

As I look back now, and see so many things that have happened in my life that have changed things for the better, but at the time things seemed impossible to cope with. You will often hear that God has a plan for all, and I can't actually understand how He can control things. But I know that He can. Whatever Satan throws at us, whatever demons present to us, as a loved child of God we will get through this. He has us in his care.

The day of the funeral was weird, and the events of that day really made me think about funerals in general. Dad was cremated, and we went to the crematorium in the funeral car. After the funeral, Uncle Phil and Nana decided to go and see where my Pa (Nan's husband) was placed. We searched and searched, but nothing could be found. Eventually they asked the curator who thought for a while, and then announced that Pa was, in fact, still in a box in his office after some 10 years. Apparently they had been writing to my dad asking what to do with the ashes, and to pay some sort of money. But they had heard nothing.

Nana fainted, and then started crying that "Percy has never been buried!"

However, even though I loved my Pa, I just couldn't stop laughing. You had to know my dad to appreciate the fact that he would see this as nothing of any importance. The upshot was that, on the day when we cremated my dad, we brought my Pa's ashes home in a box, and had another funeral the following week. His ashes are scattered in the rose garden at home.

What now remained was what to do with the house and the 'things'. The house was under a War Service agreement, and we hadn't paid much off it but, to Mum's credit, she wouldn't take a thing and gave it all to me. It was decided that the house would be rented, and that I would go and live with my aunt and uncle (Dad's brother) and their three children. Nana was distraught, but Uncle Phil said it was too much for her to take on.

A room was prepared, and down the back of their house a paddock was made for the horse. At the time I was just finishing Year 11, and had filled out lots of forms for jobs – like the bank, Myers, nursing, etc. I really wanted to do nursing at Heidelberg with my friend, so I was hopeful about that. But first I had to at least finish Year 11. I would have liked to do Year 12, but I think it was financially impossible for Uncle Phil and my new family situation.

Life at Uncle Phil's was very different. There were rules which had to be obeyed, even rules suggesting how handkerchiefs needed to be ironed and folded.

There were allocated study times when I was at home, and this was something that I had never done before. There were chores and, above all, there was to be silence when Uncle Phil came home, and no one was allowed to use his special glass which was also to be kept in the fridge. I loved my cousins very much, but affection wasn't something that was given unless it was demanded.

If they did things wrong they were smacked, and I hated that. I just couldn't handle it, even though it was none of my business. I would cry to Nana and, in the end, I begged Uncle Phil to let me go home to Nanas.

Chapter 13

The end of School and College Begins (16+)

Despite the fact that I wanted to go nursing, it was agreed that I would go to teacher's college and become a teacher, as this would mean that I would be earning money through a studentship. There was no discussion, it was just decided. I wasn't going to be a nurse after all, and save people, and marry a very rich doctor. But, OK. It wasn't so bad. In retrospect I am glad it happened, though I also wanted very much to go back to school and do Year 12. I can look back now and see the hand of God. However, at the age of 16, teacher's college provided me yet another round of insecurity.

It was probably at this time that I began to really look at my own sexuality, and wonder exactly what was happening. Although I was younger than the other girls in my year, I knew that suddenly I was looking at boys in the class differently, and had even taken a punt once on telling this one guy I fancied him, only to be rejected. This added to my already lack of confidence and anxiety.

Academically, I wasn't all that flash at college but, in fairness to myself, I never really studied. On the practical side of teaching though I constantly gained 'A's, and remained in the top 10 percent for teaching. For me, these years were strange indeed. I had a couple of boyfriends during my college years, but none that stand out, except for a boy in high school whom I really liked.

This lasted for a couple of weeks, and I got to actually play the game called 'I'm going with …' I am not all that sure why we broke up, in fact not really sure that I was a legitimate player in the 'I am going with …' game, but it all came to a head on graduation night and the relationship ended. It was assumed that, after the Graduation Ball, we would all go to a local surf beach with our boyfriends, and spend the night. I had no intention of being at the beach with him, and hadn't mentioned it. I don't think he was too happy, after bringing me home, to find me shooting out the back of my house to be picked up by my friends, considering I had told him that I was going home to sleep. Anyway that was the end of that.

What I did know during these formative years was that I was very lonely. I had no one really to talk to about life – sex boyfriends, etc – and, in front of my girlfriends, I had to pretend to be a least savvy in all of these areas. But, in fact, I wasn't. There would often be nights when I would lie awake in bed wondering what my future would be. Would I get married, have children, be normal, etc? I never really knew. Living with my aunt and uncle for a short time, however, brought out something that changed everything. My aunt was really concerned that, at 16, I hadn't started menstruating. So, at her insistence, examinations needed to be done. I was packed off to see Dr Woods, and was scheduled to have an internal to investigate whether I had a womb, or anything at all.

Dr Woods had been my family doctor for years and, although he was a little rough, I trusted him until he asked the question, prior to the examination, "Have you ever had sex with a boy, or been fingered by a boy?" This was his question.

I was mortified! "How dare you!" I yelled!

His attitude changed immediately, and he patted my shoulder saying, "It's okay. I'm sorry. Of course you haven't."

I saw the dragon (his assistant) smile to herself, and then at me, indicating that she thought I was lying. I never really liked her much, and this time I liked her even less.

Woodsy explained what he was going to do, and how the dragon would be there helping me. My mum had also been called upon for the main event, which was strange, but she also stood there motionless. I can't recall anything much, except this pressure below, and then I started screaming. It was like screaming in a nightmare. I couldn't hear the sound, but I was in excruciating pain and I think I was turning blue. The nurse slapped my face. (I figured she would have enjoyed that!)

Dr Woods left the room, and my mother just stood there. I was howling and sobbing, and my mum's comforting words were: "Don't worry love. You get used to it. That's just what happens when you have sex!"

I looked at her in astonishment, and then promised myself that I would never have sex or get married!

Dr Woods came back and said that he was unable to do the examination properly. It was decided that I would go to the hospital and have an internal while I was also having my tonsils out. However, he did feel that he had found a womb, but we needed to be sure.

I lay in the hospital bed, my throat was sore, I couldn't swallow and, between my legs, there was a thick pad of gauze. The nurse entered the room, pulled back the blanket and, with a younger girl in tow, bellowed, "Get his creature cleaned up immediately. She's obviously menstruating!"

Stupid woman! I was bleeding and hurting as the hymen had been cut. Once again proving how stupid and incompetent hospital personnel can be.

They entered like a military trial – Dr Woods, Mum, Nana, and Aunty Shirley.

"Well!" said Woods. "We have success. We certainly found a womb, and I have cut the hymen as it was incredibly thick. So now, when your time is right, they can poke a lamppost up there and you won't feel a thing."

Nice comment, eh!

"Told you," Mum said, glaring at Aunty Shirley. "She's just like me, a late bloomer." Nana was the only one who came forward and gave me a cuddle.

"I am so hungry, Nan," I said.

Bending down she told me that I was not able to eat anything for a while with my tonsils out, but she had left chocolates in the draw and I could suck the middle out of the them. Good old Nana! "Don't tell anyone though!" she said, and winked at me.

Chapter 14

———

I am a teacher

Hard to believe, but I finally graduated and started life as a teacher. I entered a secondary school in March as the Phys Ed teacher, at the ripe old age of 17 turning 18. Somehow I had survived the early stages of my life, and was embarking on a new career. I had a studentship so could, to some degree, support myself. I was living at Nana's, had good friends, and played lots of sport. So I was always busy. Even boys now started to interest me a little, but they still frightened me.

At this stage, from a sexual point of view, I had further tests and was now taking the pill and menstruating regularly. I understood also that the likelihood of not having children was high as my ovaries were not producing properly but, to some degree, this didn't bother me too much. Everything seemed to be there, and finally boobs started to develop, or at least little bumps. From a point of view of trying to understand why panic and anxiety play such an important part of my life, when I look back this era seems my most content. Yet was it?

The days were full, life was okay with Nan, but I was so lonely. Friends were there, and they were great, but I had carefully scripted what each friend knew of my life. It became a constant battle to ensure that I never messed up, or related things that each particular friend did not know.

I was so lonely, and the nights were long and full of bad dreams. Even recently my husband says that he found me curled up in bed, yelling out to Nana to come and get me. There were a few boys involved in my life, and sometimes I would fantasize just what Mr Right would look like. I would think about the guys I knew, about what life would be with each of them, and play family games in my head. I hated the school holidays as these were the times that I was very much alone, and the times that the various sport competitions were in recess.

The only solace I had was my life with God, and church became my consistent haven.

Despite my ups and down, I had this weird sense that God had put me on the Earth for a reason and that, despite some strange occurrences in my life, somehow He was always there, and somehow I survived.

But then it changed.

"Do you want to dance?" he said. I was standing by the pole at the local dance, in my beautiful white coat with my nose in the air. I looked up and saw him there. I had known him forever, as he was my best friend's brother. He usually gave me a hard time when I spent time at her place.

Previous to his request, his friend had asked me to dance, and I had replied, "Go away, you nit. Why would you think that I would dance with you?"

As you can see, I had a wonderful way with dealing with suitors.

My reply to this request was in the same vein, "Why would you think I would dance with you when I wouldn't with your stupid mate?"

His reply was simple: "Because, if you don't, you won't last the game on court next week!"

He was an umpire, and often umpired our division one women's games.

That was it. We took the dance floor. The dance finished; the night was over.

"Get your coat," he said. "I'll take you home." Not another word was spoken. I got my coat, walked down the stairs, and there he was. We walked outside. In a car his mate was waiting with his girlfriend.

"Get in," he said. I did. While sitting on the back seat, a bottle of beer was passed to me, along with hot chips in a packet. I had a swig, ate some chips, and that was it. Very romantic!

We got to my house, he walked me to the door, kissed me goodnight, and then said: "I'll pick you up tomorrow. We're going on a barbecue."

Four years later we were engaged, and then married the following year.

He was and is my rock, my one sense of normality. Not able to understand the depression or panic that occurs, but always there to pick up the pieces.

Somehow he just moved into our lives, Nan and mine, and became as familiar with my family as I was.

He virtually became part of the furniture at our place. Yes, there were ups and downs in the relationship and, for me, I still struggled with thoughts of where I belonged, and was I good enough. And what about the marriage bit, and having, or not, having our own children. His advice was simple. We would have lots of fun trying, and just see what happened. His life was so normal and, while once I had loved going to his house as his sister's friend, now things became difficult. Families scared me, and I wondered if they thought I was good enough. So where I could, I avoided most personnel contact.

I imagined that life with this new love in it, and home with Nana, might go on until we got married, but once again I was faced with an old enemy.

Life remained settled, and he settled into the family and virtually became part of it spending most weekends with Nana and I. I never really thought about the fact that Nan was a pensioner, and existed on a minimum wage.

Begrudgingly each week I would hand over $10, which I naturally expected would cover all my board, food, laundry, and more, as well as Keith's weekend stays.

To say I was lazy around the house was an understatement, and my bedroom was always a mess, with saddles and horse stuff along with sports stuff. Clothes littered the floor and, if they made it to the laundry basket, then the expectation from me was that they would be washed ironed and returned with a 24-hour cycle.

Nan also cared for her brother, a man I called 'Twinkle' as he was always dancing around, usually drunk. Twinkle used to be an A-grade electrician, and there were times when people from Fords would come and get him, sober him up and take him to the factory, as he was one of the few men that knew the wiring there.

He also had his own band that played at the Palais, and was an excellent pianist. He was to be married, but got jilted by his fiancée. From there things just went downhill for him.

Even though she had 10 brothers and sisters, none of them would take him in except my Nan. Twinkle had a bed in the garage, which was loaded with blankets. He was so skinny. From pension day, until he ran out of money, you wouldn't see him, but usually in the last four days, he would come inside for meals and hog the fireplace. The day he came, and ended up staying, I remember well. It was raining, and the police brought him to the front door. He was soaking wet, and had been to see my nanna's sister who lived in Newton, but she had refused to take him. He came inside that night, and there he stayed.

My nana used to boss him around, and actually threw him around like a rag doll, but he would just say: "Don't upset yourself, Pearl!" He would come inside drunk and be singing and dancing, and Nana would do her block.

Sometimes she would watch him waddle down the lane with his bottle of sherry, or find bottles in his room, and would take them. Nana never drank but, when she died, we found about two dozen bottles of sherry in her wardrobe. I remember one day she grabbed him, and the bottle he had in his hand, and pulled him to the gully trap. She held him there while she poured out the sherry. Twinkle cried like a baby, sobbing, "You are taking my blood, Pearly. Don't do it!"

It was so funny. On one occasion I was coming home from town in the tram, and noticed he was up the back. He was singing, and carrying on like a pork chop, and people were laughing at him. As he walked past me to get off the tram, he doffed his hat and said: "Good evening, Madam!" refusing to acknowledge me at all.

People used to call him "Nature's gentleman" and the police would often bring him home, or call Nana to get him from the lock-up.

So there was my life – Nana, Twinkle, my soon-to-be husband, and me. Life seemed wonderful and very normal, but things were about to change.

Chapter 15

Death Again

Racing home from teaching, and in a hurry to get to basketball and catch up with Keith and my friends, I was tearing around getting ready and about to make it into the shower.

"Get me a cup of tea, will you, fatso," I bellowed through the shower curtain.

"Always running," I heard her reply. "One of these days, my girl!"

I heard the crash, a deep sickening thud. As I turned and walked out of the bathroom, I could see Nana on the ground, lying on her back. I raced towards her screaming, "Get up, Nan! Get Up!"

I looked at her face, and saw her smile. I could do nothing but hold her and kiss her, as the tears streamed down my face. She looked so peaceful. I know I should have done compressions, mouth-to-mouth, whatever, but

I just didn't and I don't know why. To this day, one of my demons always reminds me how I killed her, and how hopeless I am.

I just held her, and sobbed, until I knew she wasn't there anymore. Sometimes I blame myself for not acting as I should and, if I had, maybe Nan would have lived longer.

I can't remember the order of things, but I rang people I thought I should. I called the ambulance, the doctor (who wasn't answering), and then called my Uncle Phil (Nan's son, who kind of looked after us). Everyone seemed to come at once.

The doctor rang back and yelled at me to stay off the phone in future, because this could have saved Nana, a comment that adds even now to my guilt. But I don't remember ever getting a list of instructions of what to do when someone dies.

With all this happening Twinkle walked in, doffed his hat, and announced: "The Chief is dead." And left.

The ambulance people laid Nana on the couch, and said they had to wait for a doctor. They asked if I had special clothes to put on her. I said no, she was to be buried in her apron. Nan used to say: "When I go out of this world, I will go out picking up after you, my girl!"

There was a discussion about this, along with the fact that her rings should be taken off her and given to someone, as they could be stolen. I insisted that they be buried with her, and no one was to touch them. That she would also be buried in her apron. I must have sounded pretty author-itarian, as no one questioned me.

While all this was going on, I remembered that Nana had said to me that, if anything happened to her, just get the bells, the walking stick, the elephants, and her fur coat, and hide them immediately after she died. She claimed her sister, Lillian, would come looking for them. I left the death scene, grabbed her coat, bells, elephants, and walking stick, and raced to the woodshed. I hid them under a pile of wood.

I wasn't too worried about Aunty Lily coming to get them then, as I hadn't told her that Nana had died, but I didn't think about the fact that Twinkle would have told his sister, Lily, already.

When I came back, who was standing there bawling, but Aunty Lilly, grabbing and squeezing me, and crying heavily. Between the sobs, she gazed at me and said: "I had better get the bells, the walking stick, and the elephants. I may as well take Pearl's fur coat, as I am sure she'd want me to have it."

I suggested she look in the wardrobe for the coat, and take whatever else she wanted from the lounge room that she felt should stay with the Kelly family. Other business went on and, after a short time, Aunty Lily came back announcing that she wasn't able to find the things that she was looking for. She glared straight at me, almost accusing me of stealing the treasures.

Fortunately, Uncle Phil got into the act, and pointed out that this was not the time to be accusing anyone of anything. Incidentally, he got them all in the end and I have no idea where they are now, only that Aunty Lily didn't get anything.

Turns out that Nan knew she was going to die, had labelled everything in the top room with a Band-Aid, and attached names to the things she treasured.

In all the drama, I had forgotten about the basketball and so called a taxi to get there. I wanted to tell Keith what had happened. I walked into the stadium just as his coach was calling a 'time out'. I saw the look of wonder on his face as I marched up to the huddle, and announced: "Nan's dead. Can you come home as soon as you can?"

I didn't wait for a reply just left and went back home. Afterwards he asked me to never announce anything like that to him again, and he suggested other things I could say, like passed away, has left us, etc.

As an aside to all this, and to explain Keith's unique way of handling death, I need to show just how frightened he is of saying the word "death". When his brother-in-law, Harvey, died, Keith was asked by his sister to ring her husband's old basketball pals to let them know he had died, and to explain what arrangements were being made for the funeral.

I listened with interest as he rang each basketball family. One he had to ring was a friend of mine, whose husband was away, but she would not have known Harvey at all. The conversation went something like this:

"Hi, Cath. Just ringing to let you know that we lost Harvey today! Please, if you could let Ben know, that would be good."

After a long silence, the reply was: "Oh, that's a shame. What time did he go missing? Sometimes they can come back just on their own, so don't give up hope."

Cathy told me afterwards that she didn't understand why Keith would want Ben to know that the dog, or cat, (she wasn't sure which) was missing. I can't imagine what he is going to say when I die…

With the passing of Nan, once again, I am out on a limb. Where will I go, and how will I keep this relationship with Keith going? I never once thought of going it alone, even though I was 20, earning a wage, and was pretty sensible. What would I do now? I was running out of people to live with.

Chapter 16

Mum to the Party

The thought of living with Mum never crossed my mind, but obviously it did her's. She had been at home with my other Nana, and free from her schizophrenia for about 12 months. I saw them regularly, but it wasn't until Mum, raised the question the day after the funeral. It had been decided that I would go back to my Uncle Phil's, and live with them (outside of my consideration of course), and that the house would be sold.

The ironical thing was that the house was left to me, and to my uncle. I don't think he really approved of me having a half share.

When Mum suggested that we live together, I thought this would be a good idea. I thought that we could just stay in Nana's house (of which I owned half) and life would continue on. This was not to be. Uncle Phil wanted the money, and so the house had to be sold. I knew nothing about real estate and loans. That was when Mum was working as a domestic for a family, and they had a house to rent, so she suggested that we live there. I was happy with this, and so the York Street home was sold.

I got all the practical stuff, like fridge, cutlery, washing machine, etc. Uncle Phil took all the other stuff, like the McQueen platform rocker, the rocking horse, the bells, the walking stick, and also my Pa's Lodge belt with all his medals. The belt was the only thing that I was not happy with. Aunty Lily got the piano as she claimed it belonged to her brother, and he owed her money.

In all of the divvying up of the spoils, one thing was forgotten... Twinkle. I saw his face as he begged me to take him with me. I just couldn't. I had selfishly tried to keep what I had of my life with Nana and Keith in tack, and he didn't fit in.

Once again I felt I was responsible for another human being's life, and I had messed it up. About two months later, at the home for old men that I put him in, he died in his sleep. It really wasn't a home; it was just a room. He had been on methylated spirits before, and I visited him in hospital but, this time after he was released, he got back on the turps and that was the end.

I didn't find out until after he was buried and, for a while after that, felt worthless and horrible, given that I could have done something. But I had selfishly threw him out. In a sense, I killed him.

Life with Mum was easy and, I have to say, she was brilliant. She never once hit the grog, and took her medication regularly. We had lots of fun and, although she knew that I loved a drink and smoke, she never cracked on that I did both of these things. It was a strange mother/daughter relationship. I was free to do anything, and was never questioned about what I was doing. In some ways, though, I was still the mother. I told her what to do, and constantly made sure that she understood if she ever went out and got drunk, she would never come back. Keith was made extremely welcome. She adored him and knitted him cricket jumpers every year. For two years, life went on here. Now I was 24, and about to get married.

The day dawned and it was clear that it was going to be hot. I had a hangover from the girl's night out, and wasn't feeling all that well. After we all had our hair done, I decided to have a lay down in the back room. I really couldn't cope with much more.

Mum's wig didn't match the colour of her hair, and one of the brides-maids wanted to get her hair redone with her own hairdresser. I was over it, so I took myself off for a rest.

I awoke to screaming and panic, as they couldn't find me and thought I had run away. The photographer was there, and I wasn't even dressed. Things somehow got done; photos were taken, and off we went to the church.

The service was fine, along Methodist lines. I had never seen Keith look so pale; in fact he was grey. Beads of perspiration ran down his face, and the minister gave him a handkerchief on which he duly blew his nose. As we proceeded to the outer vestry to sign the register, he planted his foot on my train and I couldn't move, despite his constant whispers of "Move! Move!"

Finally reaching the vestry, the minister announced that my husband could now kiss me. In front of the minister, he announced that he just wanted to get out of there, and that he would never ever go through this again.

It was at the reception he hit his straps, and became the social monster that he is. He enjoyed it immensely, while I was in conversation with the caterers as to how much the guests were drinking. We started off with four waiters and, by 9.00pm, I had cut it down to two. I was paying for all this, and I had a budget.

My brother-in-law jokingly said he had never seen a bride so anxious to leave early. The reason? It was costing me a fortune, and they were drinking like fishes .... not what he believed the reason to be.

The wedding ended, much to my husband's annoyance, and we set off on our honeymoon. To add to the drama of the day, when we arrived at the motel he realised that we had left the cheque book behind!

We had a great time after leaving the posh hotel in Adelaide and, after four days, headed to Mildura through the Barossa Valley. Having sampled much of the wine on the first day of our journey, we were forced to sleep in the car! We loved Mildura so much that for 25 years it became our Christmas holiday vacation, and even today we often reminisce about the 'Good Old Days'. Married to a wonderful person, and now a teacher with a degree, I thought I had life made. I knew nothing of panic and depression. and I seemed to be able to cope with many things without missing a beat.

After the wedding, Mum had a breakdown, and was committed to Parklands.

In Parklands she had met a man called Kevin, who became my step-father. You can imagine how thrilled I was about this, as 'Kevy Boy' had his own mental demons. I could never understand why the staff there had encouraged the relationship, but she was over 21, and a widow.

Mum and her new husband, Kevin, moved in to look after my grandfather.

Between the three of them I was constantly in demand. It all came to a head when Mum and her father had a fight after spending the afternoon drinking beer. When I say fight, I mean 'fight'!

Pop had a black eye, and Mum had a swollen jaw. Mum and Kevin had taken off with their belongings and had left Pop. Naturally I was called, brought Pop home, and put him to bed in our house. About two hours later, Mum arrived. It appeared that she and Kevin had also had a fist fight, and Mum had left him. I put Mum into the spare bed, and then it started. They both began yelling at each other. I couldn't handle much more of this, so I let fly and slammed both their doors shut, threatening to call the police and have them evicted if they didn't shut up.

In the morning things had calmed down, and it appeared that Mum had belted Kevin because he had hit Pop, and so Pop was quite thrilled that Mum had stuck up for him, regardless of the black eye she had given him earlier.

It was only a matter of time before Kevin came back on the scene. Life went along OK for a while, until Mum had a really bad episode and finished up in Parklands yet again.

Pop had called me by to come and get her and, when I arrived, I could see she was completely off the planet. With a bag of snowballs in hand, I convinced her to come with me to the hospital where we would be able to get some more medication that would stop the voices.

Off we went! Sitting in the waiting room things changed. After eating most of the snowballs, Mum stood up in front of everyone and, pointing to me, announced, "You! You bitch! It's all your fault. I've hated you since the time you were in my belly!" I stood up, and then she hit me in the face.

I was used to the abuse, and sometimes the physical slap, but could usually predict what was happening. This time I couldn't! I slapped her back as hard as I could, and yelled at her to never ever hit me again! It was a sort of automatic response and, to this day, I regret that I ever hit her.

The waiting room was still! Not a sound could be heard. I had never spoken to my mother like that.

"Oh, you are my little Chicko," she said. "My beautiful daughter! How about some more snowballs?"

Mum never hit me again, despite the fact that there were many more times I would have to intervene.

On one occasion I found her in a Kombi van, with a Negro man. They were both naked, not a nice sight as my mother was a very large lady. I tried to pull her out, screaming at her, but she refused to go. Giving up in the end, I turned to the guy and said, "You must find it rewarding, fucking someone who is mentally incapable of even thinking logically."

He was not happy, and told me if I didn't go he would make sure that I would never see my mother again, and with that he produced a knife. I ran out of the yard, down to Pakington Street, and decided that never, again, would I go seek her out when she was having one of her episodes. I had a life, and a son I had to protect and take care of.

Mum and I never spoke about it, and nothing was ever mentioned when she was around during her good times. It was as though these sorts of things didn't really happen, and that we, her family, were making it up

I now realise how much trouble I could have been in. I can look back now and see the hand of God protecting me, though at the time I never realised this.

As another example of the delusional dramas with Mum that I had to deal with, two policemen appeared at my door, demanding to see my son's birth certificate. She had told them that my son was actually hers, and that I had taken him and was trying to drown him in our pool. She could be so convincing in this state, and the cops made me go and get the birth certificate to prove we had adopted him. What didn't look good was that we had a large concrete pool in the back yard...

We existed in this wacky environment until my pop finally passed away (see, I am learning!). He had been ill, and was in Grace McKellar House, a Geelong rehabilitation hospital and centre for the aged. Despite this, he would try and escape and make his way to our house in Belmont, where he would precede to mow the lawns, trying to show me that he was useful and could live with us.

What was I to do? He was incontinent and sometimes very forgetful, and I had a six-month-old baby. I walked in one day and found him fondling the baby's genitals, and that was it. I loved my Poppa, but I couldn't do this anymore. He had a son and I rang him, but he told me not to ring him again until he was dead. As far as he was concerned, Pop could live in the gutter.

On returning to the hospital, I think Pop sort of gave up. He went into a coma, and died about three weeks later. They phoned me and suggested that, if treatment was stopped, then the angels would come and take him, probably that night. I went in, and stayed with him until they came.

Chapter 17

———

Life as an Educator, and Motherhood.

During my first 10 years of teaching, life seemed really normal. I loved my job, my social life was good, and married life was also great. Sure, we had our ups and downs, as most couples do. We had built our first home and, while it wasn't exactly finished, it was liveable. While there we managed to save money while it was being completed.

My husband's job which, we had thought, would be safe forever, was about to come to an end, and this forced him into a situation where he had to go away to South Australia to work. I think this put probably the greatest strain on our marriage, as he only got home every second or third week. In the school holidays I would go up there, and we would stay in a caravan for the two weeks.

I was lonely and, I am sure, he was too, and so we sought solace in our friends. There were dramas and problems that sent me into a spin, some involving school, and others just in my personal life. As our marriage went on, it became apparent that I would never be pregnant, and so we applied for adoption.

After a six year wait, and a few mis-matches, the call came to pick up our beautiful baby boy. I wanted to call him Luke John, but my husband insisted that was far too religious. He insisted that he be named Mark Andrew, little realising they, too, were disciples.

Both my beautiful children were adopted, and they became our joy and delight. Normality finally seemed to exist, but that wasn't to be. As a mother I was really hopeless! Not having brothers or sisters, and not really ever having anything much to do with children, I had no idea at all.

My daughter has seven beautiful kids, and I watched with delight as she so capably raised each of them. On the other hand, I really struggled. As an example, I remember going shopping. Knowing I would only need a few things, I put my beautiful baby boy in the pusher, and started walking around the supermarket. Having browsed around, I put the groceries in the car, and then drove home. Pulling up outside out house, and reaching for the grocery bags, I noticed that the car seat was vacant.

"Oh, no!" I cried. I had left him in the supermarket!

On returning to the shop, there he was in the pram. Smiling away to these faces all peering at him.

Even my beginning into motherhood had a strange start. We had to pick him up, and bring a set of new clothes to change him into. I had to change his nappy, and put the new clothes on him. Something I had never done before. I don't think people realise that, after waiting a long time and missing out on a number of possible kids through mothers changing their minds, you suddenly get a phone call and, bingo, the next day there you are.

As I began this new adventure, I looked up at Keith and casually said, "He's got a rough looking head!" Just as I said this, his penis shot up and bang! Right in my face I coped a soaking.

"That's just exactly what you deserve," Keith said, laughing at me. "There's nothing wrong with his head."

The only new born baby I had ever seen was my best friend's daughter, Linda (Looby Lo), who is my God-daughter. I will swear that she was born without one single wrinkle, and that her hair was combed and parted down one side. My Marko had a fat round face, red spots from the medication he had been given, and a mass of red unruly hair.

He was the most beautiful baby, and grew into the most handsome man.

I was lucky though. Without brothers and sisters to help me, God had supplied me with my best friend, Annie, who lived next door. I called her 'Mother'. She had four kids of her own, and was a nurse. But, above all, she understood me, and would protect me from anything.

Even when I was wrong she would find something positive in my actions. I once gave Mark a Butternut Snap biscuit when he was about six months old, as he was crawling around and annoying me. A couple of times I looked at him, and he looked strange. Finally I could see he was going blue, and couldn't breathe. I picked him up and ran into Anne's. She quietly turned him upside down, put her fingers down his throat, and pulled out a ball of biscuit. I was a mess, but she quietly told me that it was fine, that it could happen to anyone and no harm was done. There were so many times that she was there for me, and minded him when I decided to go back to work for a couple of days per week as we needed the money.

For some 10 years we all holidayed together in Mildura with the kids. Anne got MS, and died after two years. I did her eulogy, and told everyone the story of Annie's Angels. This was something she told me that had happened to her when she was a young student nurse living in Norlane. She was walking down the street one night when four boys surrounded her, and threatened to rape her.

An angel appeared, wrapped his wings around her, and they ran away. You may think this is a little crazy, but Anne was not a Christian, and we never talked about God. She begged me not to tell anyone about this as she didn't understand it, but I think I did. Annie was sent by God to teach me how to become a mother and, in the eulogy, I told her story and realised how blessed I was to have her as my friend. I have chosen this one incident with the biscuit, but I could have written about so many times Anne was my rock and strength, and I loved her dearly.

Anne was the example I had of motherhood, and what a good mother should be.

As a child I was confused. I couldn't understand really why Mum did some of the things she did. As I grew up, and grew to understand more about life and God, I began to see my mum in a different light.

Chapter 18

———

What is Motherhood?

Uncle Bob saw me after my mum's funeral, and said, with a smile on his face: "Don't do my eulogy, Chick, because it will take too long!" I think it was his way of telling me that he thought Mum's eulogy was far too long, but I was determined her story would be told.

The reason I think I wanted to tell the story was that finally, in death, I realised just how strong my mother was, and just how much she had actually loved me.

I am not going to relate the whole thing, but just this important part. I hope it tells you how wrong I was about my mum. All her life she had suffered from schizophrenia, which was beyond her control and, as a result, found herself in terrible situations. At these times she did not have the skills to look after a child. The disease was relatively new in those early days, and intervention consisted of heavy sedation – for example lithium, and Largactil, as well as shock treatment. Mum had all of these from time to time, and spent sometimes up to two years in mental institutions before being allowed out.

Her death came after two years in the Grace McKeller House, for physical rather than mental problems, and during these two years she never had a mental episode.

I got some time before the funeral to actually go away and reflect on my mum's life, and this is what I began with...

> *The poet Adam Lindsay Gordon wrote: 'Life is mostly froth and bubble, two things stand like stone. Kindness in another's trouble, courage in your own.'*

To me this quote described my mother to a tee.

My daughter, Kate, sent me a card, and in it she wrote that she would remember grandma because of her kindness. An apt and fitting description.

My mum would give you the shirt of her back, if she had it. As for courage, I am just beginning to understand just how courageous she actually was.

Her sickness meant she wasn't around much during my early years. Later in my life, she provided me with knowledge of the family that I had come from.

She linked me to my dad, and reminded me of my young days when things were happy.

My mum knew God, and knew also that she was going to Heaven. The night before she died I visited her, and she told me of dream she had had. She was walking up some stairs towards Heaven.

"Believe it or not, Nola," she said. "I don't have any pain, I just kept walking and laughing."

Mum had been in a wheel chair for two years!

All these years I had put my dad on a pedestal, and had seen him as the only one who cared. Now I just wanted to turn back the clock, and tell her that I loved her, and understood how hard things must have been for her. I have had heroes in my life, and had often felt unloved by her for not giving me the normality that I believed I deserved, but now I understood. Looking at her face, peaceful and radiant on the day she died, I knew that she understood many of the decisions that I had made as a child, and had loved me for it. I was strong, just like her. She made me strong, and she loved me, and I loved her. She was indeed my hero, and how clever was God to give me her as a mother.

It seems everyone else is an expert and, as a new mother, you feel so incompetent. But then it happens. This tiny creature smiles and gurgles, and they are yours forever with a love that knows no ending, despite whatever happens. I wondered if my mum had thought that about me, and somehow I knew that she did. Despite everything, and in spite her illness, through God's grace I had turned out OK. I had been chosen by Him, and she was indeed my mother. Together we were a family, despite the fact that so many things had happened. My children became part of this family too, and they loved their grandma.

My son became affected by heroin, and died eight years ago from an overdose. My beautiful talented baby left this world, and left me devastated and alone. I could write a book (and maybe I will) as a mother on the problems and pitfalls of dealing with this situation, and the impact it has on families.

My demons roared during this time. My strategies helped, but never completely obliterated the problem and my pain. So many times all I could say was: *"Gentle Jesus, meek and mild, look upon a little child; pity my simplicity and suffer me to come to Thee."*

I remember quite clearly one day, when Mark was doing a detox, I asked him if I could I pray for him. He smiled his beautiful smile, and agreed.

"OK, Mum. But I think we can assume God has protected me from cot death as I'm 35."

Every night I would pray this prayer over my kids before they went to sleep, and my heart leapt as I knew he remembered me doing it.

"May the Lord bless you, and keep you from the cot death, and all the trials and troubles of the night, and help you love the Lord Jesus with all your heart and soul."

I was obsessed with the cot death. Mark knew God, and God knew Mark, and despite all the problems, as a family we still ate at the table. My daughter loved her brother, and made sure her kids loved him also.

Maybe one day I can write about him, and the troubled times we went through.

I have to say that I would never have coped without God in my life. Somehow, dealing with this drug addiction, I realised how that in my life

I had coped with many situations, and my faith in God (limited as it was), would see me through. This made living possible, although there were some times when I felt I was drowning.

Mark's death was certainly something that hit me hard, and something that took me many times to the pit, screaming: "Why God, why me? Why did You let that happen?" Yes, it's still horrible, but I know there is an end and, by using the strategies I have developed, and by drawing close to God, I will get through any attack, even his death.

I understand it's OK to grieve and to feel bad, but I also understand now that this will ease. God will protect me, as He always has, and eventually I will find peace again. I know that I loved Mark. I did my best and, yes, I have been through the 'if only I had ...' stuff.

My best advocate was Mark himself, who would constantly tell me that he loved me. That it wasn't my fault, that we were great parents, and he couldn't have wished for better. It's hard for anyone to understand the grief one feels for the loss of a child unless they have been through it. And many sit in judgement about what they would have done.

My beautiful daughter has her own demons to face. Unlike Mark, she is independent and strong. She is nothing like me at all and, for that, I am glad, as I'm sure she is too. She is, without a doubt, the best mum in the world, and people tell me that she is a great nurse as well. I could not have asked for anyone better.

She gave me the greatest gift ever when she asked me to come to the birth of my first grandchild. For someone who could never have kids, this was the most wonderful thing I have ever seen. I watched in amazement as my Bailee came into the world, and was astonished as to how brave and magnificent my daughter was.

The midwife gave me the job of watching the monitor, and telling her when the contractions were coming. I did this with a sense of urgency. Finally realising that she knew when they were coming, I was told to watch for the delivery. The pain must have been terrible so, in my usual manner, I decided to sing "Jesus loves me this I know, for the Bible tells me so".

"Mum," came the response. "I think we can stop with the God stuff!"

Finally, my little alien was born, and I got to hold her. Love at first sight, as it was with all six, though I didn't go to all their actual births. One was enough! But I was there immediately after each one, except for the last one. My Prince Harry.

I found it so hard, just watching the beautiful daughter in my life go through such pain, and not being able to do anything to help her, or fix it. But such joy watching her holding these beautiful bundles in her arms, not once but six more times.

How blessed was I? The one without a family now had seven beautiful grandchildren, all thanks to my Kate. God had certainty blessed me greatly.

In some ways I think I am a disappointment to Kate. I am never really sure as we disagree on many things. I would often get myself into such state about some of the things she says, but now I am learning to say to myself that it's not my problem anymore. She is capable of making her own decisions, and doing her own thing. Just as I did.

However, Mark was my constant worry with his addiction. There are times when I look back and think I should have paid more attention to Kate, and what she was feeling. Hindsight is a wonderful thing, isn't it. When your kids are hurting, you just put all your effort into the hurt one.

I have done my best as a parent, to be a good mum to my kids and grandchildren. How they will judge me in my role as grandparent and mother in my final year, I don't know. I have no control over that. I certainly haven't been perfect, and sometimes it has been this relationship that has sent me into depression. This allows my demons to roar. As usual though God has been there, carried me through, and allowed things to pass.

So many times I have cried: "Why God? Why me?" But then I can look back and see that, in all things, He has not 'quenched the burning flesh'.

Even now I can see that, with all that has happened, God was with me, and He never gave me anything that would destroy me.

My mother was a schizophrenic, my son was addicted to heroin, and Kate made a bad choice in her first marriage. With all of this, there was love between us. Kate and Mark loved each other as brother and sister, and I was so blessed that, despite the many situations that arose (and believe me there were many), the dining room table was always a place where we could all meet and be together. Kate was incredible. Given her brother's addiction, she never once restricted his access to the kids, and he would never have put the kids into any form of harm. Even today they talk about Uncle Mark, how wonderful he was, and how much fun.

People that know Kate sing her praises. She is a wonderful nurse, and has made some beautiful friends who have supported her. Her children are her priority, and they all love her dearly. With seven of them she has made sure that, whatever her circumstances, they are the priority of her life. I marvel at the way she remains calm, despite the many circumstances she has had to face. In some ways she is my rock, and I wish I could be more like her.

Chapter 19

A Reflection

I have read many books from famous people telling of their lives, and the problems they had, and how they moved through these problems. I guess, because they are famous, it seems more interesting than my life. Who really would care about an ex-principal and her life. Who had achieved nothing more than just being a wife, mother, and worker?

I was fascinated with Jimmy Barnes and his story about growing up, and how difficult his life was. But, I was envious in a way because, although he was poor and his parents fought, he had a home, with brothers and sisters. He could always seek refuge with friends, and then come home. How often I had wished for a brother, a sister, or anything in those early years, and even today still do. The fact remains that, famous or not, all of us have a unique story to tell.

How amazing life is, and how resilient we humans are. For me it had to be someone who held my life together, and was in charge of my destiny. My Nana had told me, from a very early age, that that someone was Jesus.

I took hold of that, and just hung onto it with the simple faith of a child through my prayer "Gentle Jesus, meek and mild, look upon a little child; pity my simplicity, and suffer me to come to Thee."

Although there were times when I rejected Him, and became angry with Him for what I had to go through, I could not deny His existence. I remember when my dad died, I came home from the hospital and got every Bible I could find and burnt them in anger, screaming: "I hate You. You're not real. How could You let this happen to me when, for the first time ever, I had a real life?"

Today I have my demons – anxiety, depression, and what I call my 'gloom and doom' master. I struggle with parenting. Why, because I was never parented, never protected, in any tangible way never loved as a child except by my grandparents. But now I have Jesus, and through my knowledge of Him and His word, I am the conqueror. They still come... but I have a way of putting on the whole armour of God, and I can work through them with His guidance.

Any love I received came from achieving. My achievements in sport were recognised, as were my achievements in school, but the expectations set for these achievements had to be exceptionally high. I remember playing netball when I was about 12, and I was filling in for a senior team, well above my age group. I got flattened by a large girl, and I lay on the asphalt with my legs bleeding. As I looked up, I saw my father appear from behind a tree. I didn't even know that he was watching. He walked towards me so that I could hear, and whispered: "Get up off the ground. You can't win a game from there!"

Growing up people would say that I was aggressive on the basketball court, and even on the tennis court. I like to win, win at all costs. Of course, now I can see this comes from the fact that, in order to get love or approval, I had to win. The downside of this is the fact that, when I don't win, an opportunity exists for my demons to come flooding in, and depression races to the forefront, telling me I am a failure.

I guess winning also applied to school. I had to try and be the best, the best teacher, the best principal, etc. The other point that I need to explain was that, in striving to be the best, I made enemies. The adverse of this was, of course, that I wanted everyone to like me, so that cut against the grain and usually brought on anxiety. On the surface it appears that I am strong, and can cope with anything, but underneath I always become very hurt and, again, this provides space for my demons.

Chapter 20

———

The Message

The message that I want to give is that, despite the fact that things look as though they are stacked against you, you can survive. I have learnt, and am still learning, how to deal with my demons, but writing this and realising the background that I had, I am starting to see that I am a magnificent creature of God's creation. I can recognise my demons better now, from understanding my beginnings and, in recognising them, I deal with them much better.

Looking back over many things I realise that I did what I did because I was a child. I wanted to go home with Nana, and not stay and wait for Mum. That decision by me, as a child, was a good one. I made my way when Dad died, and then Nana. And those decisions turned out to be right.

By coming home with Mum, and moving out of the house after Nana died, which left her brother, Maurice (the town drunk), no place to go, allowed my demons to surface and scream at me: "See you are evil. You deserve to be punished. You will go to court, and the judge will find you guilty!"

Now I understand that Jesus has paid the price for my sin. In doing so, I have no guilt, because Jesus lives in my heart and so I am free. I'm not going to court, or to jail, so Satan has no power over me.

The early life that I experienced, allowed me to cope with many things. My psychologist explained that I over-think things far too much, but she also said that this over-thinking was also a protection mechanism, and often kept me safe. Yet another gift from a loving God.

I have learnt to recognise that these accusations occur when I am under pressure to achieve, and feel failure. I am learning to cut them off at the beginning by knowing the times when they may possibly appear.

These include, losing a game, anger, arguments, frustrations, not getting my own way, being criticised for doing what I think is right. For you they may be more specific, like hunger, tiredness, or loneliness. One of the worst times is when that I perceive that someone doesn't like me. These are the times when I feel anxiety or depression taking a hold so, when they occur, I start to make sure that I am really busy. I will clean the house, dig the garden, take out my grandchildren, invite people for dinner, etc. Anything that makes me live in the present.

Perhaps my greatest strategy is to pray out loud, and to read God's word. During these times I will try and confirm what I understand to be true about God. I will read the Apostles Creed aloud to myself, and repeat it. I have also recorded, in my journals, many situations where God has clearly shown me things. When I have gone through the mill and then He has delivered me safely through.

It is good advice to stop and journal these things for yourself. Then, when you look back, you will see that somehow you got through this by the grace of God.

I also have a list of what I call my 'Wow Miracles!' These are the times that God has answered my prayers almost immediately. It doesn't always happen this way but, by remembering my Wow Miracles, it reminds me of just how powerful my God is, and that He can do all things. An example of these was when I left my car unattended, without a handbrake on. When I returned, I found that it had rolled across a busy street. It had backed itself between two other cars, without getting a scratch or hitting any oncoming traffic!

Another one of my Wow Miracles was when we took over as managers of a large hotel in the city. My husband insisted we live there as well, and so we packed up and moved. The day we shifted in my son (four years old) started vomiting. He was very sick, and the conditions in the pub were awful. I prayed for him to be cured and promised God that, if this was done, I would get out of there and go home. He stopped vomiting, and we went home the next day. It was clear that God did not want me to live in that particular place.

There are so many other instances on my list, like parking the car when there doesn't seem to be parks available. My grandchildren think this is hilarious, and always say: "OK, Nan. Do your God stuff with the car park." Usually God finds one…

There are too many instances to list where I can see that God has taken control of things. Sometimes it doesn't always work out the way I think it should initially but, when I look back later, I can see that it was for my own good. Making the list, and reading them when depression starts, gives me hope and confidence. It confirms, when I am at my lowest, that God has me in His arms. **Romans 8:28**.

I have found that, having someone to talk to (it might me a psychologist or a Christian friend) can help at these times. For me, one of the most dangerous times is when things are going well. Sometimes I find this difficult to accept, and will worry myself about coming events that will change this.

I find it very hard to accept normality and, when things are progressing normally, I am anticipating that the wheels are going to fall off. At these times I try very hard to change any bad thoughts from 'What if?' to 'So what?' and try to read through **Philippians 4:13** to remind myself that 'I can do all things through Christ who strengthens me'.

Sometimes I allow myself to go to the possible end of the drama in my imagination. For me this can mean going to court, and being imprisoned.

As a result of this imagined scenario, I think that everyone hates me, can see what a rotten person I really am, and how I have nothing. When this happens, I start listing all the people who will still love me, even if I am found 'guilty'. I say to myself: "My husband, my grandchildren and my best friends, Cozzie and Jan, will always love me and, above all, God will always love me and keep me safe."

Sometimes I limit myself to 15 minutes of 'worry time' and set an alarm, after which I must make myself go and do something.

While this is my strategy for coping with my severe anxiety and depression, I am not pretending that it always works immediately. But, given that today I still have to face my demons and, at 78, I can't change my early life and the things that happened to me. Nor can I blame my parents but, with the strategies that I have learnt through the years of dealing with the challenges of anxiety and depression, make sure that they do not have a ruling part of my life. I also make sure that I stay connected to God by prayer and reading His word.

Deuteronomy 31: 8 reminds me that the Lord goes before me, and will be with me, and will never forsake me, so I should not be afraid or discouraged.

While my parents weren't a real part of my upbringing, I love them both and now, as both mother and grandmother, I appreciate just how hard the job is.

There is much more to my life, but I think the important thing is to realise that I made do with what I had. I was never really a child. I never knew what it was like to have parents actually care and love me as a child. But each in their own way loved me as much as they were able.

As I said at the start, I often felt floored and wondered why on earth I was born.

Having written my story thus far I know that I had a purpose. I had chosen teaching as a career, and knew that I was a good teacher. I understood what some of these kids from poorer families felt, and I looked after people – my mum, my grandfather, and my nannas.

I cared about life and people within it. God had destined me, and given me a purpose. It wasn't going to be just teaching, and I was going to be part of His work in retirement to an extent that I would never have thought possible.

Sometimes I feel sad when I watch on television some children who have nothing. But I want to tell you that God is everything you need, even if you haven't got the right shoes, uniform, etc, and can't afford excursions. He will hold you and protect you, and prepare you for the life He has planned for you.

Chapter 21

A Retirement Job

Who would have thought, after retiring at 60 from teaching, that I would return to the work force. And who would have dreamt that I would serve God in a very direct and glorious way?

I was asked to come back to school, and take over a primary school called Whittington. Like my previous school, this one was also in a very low socio-economic area, and the principal had taken leave.

One of the first things that I did was to consolidate the Christian Religious Education program. It is basically consisted of a values program which was taught in schools in Victoria. The local minister was ecstatic, and we hit it off immediately. He ran the program, and helped me a lot by praying with me regularly about issues that were going on within the school. Not sure why it happened, but the next thing I am speaking at a conference for Christian Religious Education in a large church in Geelong, explaining how the program had assisted Whittington in achieving change.

The next thing I know I am being asked to join the organisation as a curriculum support officer, which involved working in Melbourne. As my contract at Whittington was finished, I thought about this opportunity and had a discussion with them. My job would involve writing material for children, based on Christian values, as well as a training program for volunteers to assist them to implement the program across the state. I was to have a car, expense account, office, etc. I would also be speaking in churches, and at various state functions involving CRE, as well as promoting it.

I wanted the job! But! I was not a good driver, and I had never driven to Melbourne. Despite these concerns, and after much prayer. I just said "Yes". This adventure would be much more difficult to solve than just finding somewhere to park the car. Again, God came to the rescue. The GPS helped me, but I cannot remember how many times, when I had to get onto the Bolte Bridge, I just planted my foot and cried "Just as you parted the Red Sea for Moses, please, God, part the traffic for me?"

We had many adventures, God and I, in my specially blessed car, and I managed to zoom around Melbourne and the suburbs.

I got to give talks in churches about the need for volunteer RE teachers in schools, as well as to write material for kids to use during sessions. These outlined the values of Christian education in life. I also got to work with some wonderful Christian people who provided for me both guidance and friendship. One specific friend, Dianne, I still meet regularly with in Melbourne. Her support and friendship has been invaluable. Her knowledge of the Bible, and her love for God, provides me with a wonderful example. Sometimes I had to prepare and give seminars to audiences across the various churches, and to tell my story about how God worked through my life. I actually coordinated CRE across the Barwon South Western Region, and also represented CRE in other states where our materials were sold.

People who knew me, knew that I loved God and I was a Christian. But I guess sometimes it is difficult for others, who don't really know me that well, to accept that I am a Christian, and that I believed completely in the work that I was doing. It wasn't just a job that was providing an income for us.

Again, God had me under his wing and, before the Act of Education changed and CRE became optional, I retired... for no other reason than God said: "It's over, Nola. Time to rest."

When I think of Australian Council of Christian Education, and working with them, I see it as a time when God specifically used me to do His will. Not many people get this type of opportunity and I realise now just how blessed I have been. I am just so humbled that this little kid got to live out the wonderful life that I have.

I have had to cope with many things, but I have done it through the grace of God. With my background, I am not sure if I would have coped with many of the things that happened in my later years, God had indeed taught me resilience, and prepared me for life.

I also understand a little more about predestination. I think that God gives us certain people to connect with – like families, etc – because He knows we can cope, and He chooses carefully. I also know that God has promised that He "will not quench the burning flax" and will not give us more than we can handle.

I know that, despite my upbringing, I survived. I also knew that my life going forward into old age, would never be constant. I would have to draw upon these resources and strategies to survive the onset of old age, just as I did when our family began emerging, and my children became adults. But that's for another day… maybe.

God has prepared me for whatever lies ahead and, more importantly, by connecting me with all these people – friends and family – He has used me to help His mission for the world, and for that I am grateful

Thank you, Jesus, for my life. For choosing me, and for always being there.

How could I have ever considered what started this story of mine? How could I even think of taking away my own life, when God had given me so much?

I am not famous. I'm not Jimmy Barnes, or any other famous person. I am me … a beautiful child of God, created in His image. Someone who has tried to do His will and is loved by Him.

My immortality is assured, not by my works or situations, but by his Grace through the faith I have in Him – that He is true, He is real, and He loves me.

I hope that you will find this book helpful, and find that the God I know, who loves you dearly, is your salvation. God is wonderful, and works in strange ways. This never started off to be anything more than just a recollection of things that happened in my life. A way, I hoped, that would help my grandchildren, friends, etc to understand me a little more.

I wanted to write this merely as a gift to my grandchildren, and my daughter Kate, just to show them what my life was like growing up. I hoped that, perhaps, it would explain some of my weird behaviour.

Then the reason for writing this book changed. I met a friend called Carole.

She has become another one of my 'Wow Miracles'. Carole just appeared in church, made herself known to me, explaining that she had heard that I was writing a book. I had never seen or met her before, but somehow I just knew that she was sent by God. The book, itself, had somehow lost its importance in my life, and I hadn't touched it for months.

She was an author and had just been published. She wondered if I needed any help. She agreed to read the story, and I asked her to make comments, etc and to correct (edit) my "need to use the right words!"

Within a week the manuscript came back with comments and corrections. But there was more! She thought that that the story could be used if it were altered a little. With a few alterations it could help people cope with their life situations and, more importantly, help them find God in their lives rather than to give up. I asked how I would do this, and her reply came back: "Add more God."

So, what started out as 'Ursula', and then became 'Meet My Demons', now becomes 'You are Loved'.

I hope you find this useful in your life and, please remember, you don't have to do anything, or have any special skills or talents. All you need is to believe God is God, and He has you. He has loved you from the very beginning!